50
MONEY-SAVING
TIPS
FOR EVERY
LANDLORD

A PRACTICAL GUIDE TO MAINTAINING
SHORT-TERM RENTAL PROPERTIES

MIKE McLEAN

SQUAREONE
PUBLISHERS

EDITOR: Anna Comstock
COVER DESIGNER: Jeannie Tudor
TYPESETTER: Gary A. Rosenberg
FRONT COVER PHOTO: Getty Images, Inc.
INTERIOR PHOTOS: Mike McLean

Square One Publishers
115 Herricks Road
Garden City Park, NY 11040
(516) 535-2010 • (866) 900-BOOK
www.squareonepublishers.com

Library of Congress Cataloging-in-Publication Data

McLean, Mike, 1966-
  Fifty money-saving tips for every landlord : a practical guide to maintaining short-term rental properties / Mike McLean.
      p. cm.
  Includes index.
  ISBN 978-0-7570-0352-3
  1. Rental housing—United States. 2. Landlord and tenant—United States. 3. Real estate management—United States. I. Title.
  HD7288.85.U6M375 2010
  333.33'8--dc22
                              2010002484

Copyright © 2010 by Mike McLean

Printed in Canada

10   9   8   7   6   5   4   3   2   1

Contents

Introduction, 1

 Legal Protection

Tip 1. Insulate Yourself with a Great Lease, 5

Tip 2. Take Photographs before Move-in Day, 9

Tip 3. Video Record the Entire Property, 12

 Your Business

Tip 4. Consolidate Loans into a Blanket Mortgage, 15

Tip 5. Stay Organized, 18

Tip 6. Keep Showing Your Property, 22

Tip 7. Remain Confident, 23

 Dealing with Tenants

Tip 8. Do Not Give Your Personal Phone Numbers to Tenants, 27

Tip 9. Just Say No, 29

Tip 10. Don't Spoil Good Tenants, 31

Tip 11. Don't Stress about Tenant Cleanliness, 33

⚷ Safety, Safety, Safety

Tip 12. Keep the Doors Locked, 37

Tip 13. Don't Open the Door, 38

Tip 14. Deny being the Landlord, 39

Tip 15. Always have Someone Foot Your Ladder, 40

Tip 16. Know Who You are Hiring, 41

Tip 17. Perform a Background Check, 42

Tip 18. Never Use a "For Rent" Sign, 44

Tip 19. Never Hold an Open House, 46

⚷ Interior Work

Tip 20. Quickly and Efficiently Clean Out Your Property, 49

Tip 21. Change All of the Light Fixtures, 53

Tip 22. Eliminate the Garbage Disposal, 56

Tip 23. Choose Stoves Carefully, 58

Tip 24. Remove the Dishwasher, 59

Tip 25. Remove All 220-Volt Electrical Outlets, 60

Tip 26. Replace Wall-Mounted Sinks with Vanities, 62

Tip 27. Stick to Single-Handle Faucets, 63

Tip 28. Always Use Caulk, 64

Tip 29. Hang Shower Curtains, 65

Tip 30. If the Flooring is Okay, Leave it Alone, 66

Tip 31. Think Long and Hard before Installing Carpet, 69

Tip 32. Replace Outlets and Switches, 72

Tip 33. Use Thick Sleeves to Paint, 73

Tip 34. Do Not Let Your Tenants Paint, 74

Tip 35. Make Sure the Interior Doors are Solid, 75

Tip 36. Use Structo-Lite to Repair Basement Walls, 76

Tip 37. Install Dropped Ceilings, 78

Tip 38. Limit Damage Caused by Leaks and Floods, 81

Tip 39. Prevent Roaches without an Exterminator, 84

Tip 40. Purchase these Life-Saving Tools, 86

Exterior Work

Tip 41. Do Not Grant Tenants Access to the Garage, 91

Tip 42. Choose Rubber over Tar Roofs, 97

Tip 43. Cover Windows with Plywood and Siding, 98

Tip 44. Replace Remaining Basement Window with a Hopper, 100

Tip 45. Cover the Porch Ceiling with Vinyl Siding, 102

Tip 46. Do Not Install or Repair Screens, 104

Tip 47. Remove All Shrubbery, 106

Tip 48. Make Tenants Responsible for Oil Heaters, 108

Tip 49. Switch to Cheaper Plywood, 110

Tip 50. Patch Concrete Sidewalks before Inspection, 112

Conclusion, 113

Index, 115

To Mom and Dad,
my parents,
whose unfailing support
for all my schemes and dreams
underlies each and every page of this book.

Introduction

First of all, I want to thank you for purchasing my book with your hard-earned money. Secondly, you'll be glad to know that you did not waste a cent of it! I know you work hard for your money, so if there is one thing I want you to know about me, it is that I will work even harder trying to help you save it. In fact, I'm going to save you so much cash before your Tenant even walks through the door that you're going to wish you had made this purchase a lot sooner.

Let me begin by telling you a little bit about myself. I have been a full-time Landlord in the Philadelphia area for the past fourteen years. During my first five years in the business, I acquired, renovated, and leased out over 300 homes. However, it was not all peaches and cream. I started out in this business just like everybody else. I purchased an inexpensive home, fixed it up, rented it out, and thought I was going to be the next Donald Trump. Unfortunately, it didn't quite work out that way.

I started making mistakes right out of the gate. And when you make a mistake in this business, it will cost you either time or money—two things I hate to lose! Let me tell you this, though. Whenever you jump into any line of work with no experience, you are going to make mistakes. As Oscar Wilde once said, "Experience is simply the name we give our mistakes," and for the first couple of years, I made a ton of them.

Whether it was collecting rent, installing products into my rental properties, or eliminating items from my properties before my Tenants took possession of them, I made mistakes! Oh, and did I mention that the majority of my properties were rented out to Section 8 Tenants? Section 8 Tenants are those that are issued government vouchers to cover their rent payments, and they are notorious for being the hardest Tenants to deal with. If being a bottom feeder is good for one thing in the world of Landlording, though, it's experience!

Fortunately, I'm not the kind of guy who makes a mistake and then throws his hands up in the air and quits. What I am is a thinker, and I refuse to make the same mistake twice. I thrive on coming up with inventive ways to make sure a mistake never repeats itself. Some people like to call it thinking outside the box, but I like to refer to it as very preventive maintenance.

Throughout my years as a Landlord I've had a lot of things happen to me. I've been attacked by pitbulls; I've had a guy try to fist fight me for not renting him one of my properties; I've had a Tenant run a laundromat in the basement of a property, and another run a gym from the garage. And guess what, I learned how to prevent all of these scenarios from ever happening again!

That's what this book is all about. I am going to teach you how *not* to make the same mistakes that I made. Mark Twain once said, "A man who carries a cat by the tail learns something he can learn in no other way." Well, you will never have to grab a cat by the tail because I have carried one for you! For fourteen years I have carried a cat around by the tail and taken every scratch and bite that he could dish out. I'm a better Landlord for it, and soon, you will be, too! You're getting fourteen years of my blood, sweat, and tears for less than twenty bucks. How's that for a bargain?

The way this book works is simple. I'm going to give you fifty tips—organized into six categories—that will be very beneficial to you. These are the tips that I wish I would have known when I started out in this business. They are the tips that would have saved me the most time, and of course, the most money. I will tell you the reason or story behind each tip, and in most cases, how to put my advice into action. So, without further ado, let's get started!

LEGAL
PROTECTION

TIP 1

Insulate Yourself
with a Great Lease

I believe in all of my tips, but I've put the *best* one first. Insulate yourself with a great lease. In your lease, you want to essentially state that the Tenant is responsible for everything and you are responsible for nothing. Then, make sure the Tenant signs and dates every form and piece of paper that's included in it.

A terrific lease is something that you need more than anything else to succeed in this business. However, I actually go above and beyond leases—I add addendums! The lease says everything once, and then the addendums say it all a second time in simple, understandable English.

Addendums often come in handy. For instance, let's say that some of your Tenants break a window and call you to fix it. You might instinctively refer them to page six, article twelve, paragraph nine of the lease, which states, "As my Tenant, you agree to be responsible for any items in the household that become broken by fault or no fault of your own." If they can actually find that part of the lease, you'll probably still get a, "That don't mean we have to fix your window," from the Tenants. However, with addendums your Tenants have no fight whatsoever! They are easy to locate and even easier to read. On the next page you'll see how my "Broken Window Addendum" reads.

When you make rules that clear to your Tenants, they have a choice to make. Do they go to court and try to lie their way out of the situation, or do they simply suck it up and fix the window? From my experience, 99 percent will fix the window, and the 1 percent that takes you to court will lose. Even as pro-Tenant as the

Broken Window Addendum

I _____,

the Tenant residing at _____,

take full responsibility for all windows in the property.
I understand and agree that if any windows during my
occupancy become broken, cracked or damaged in
any way, I will take full responsibility in having them
repaired at my own expense and none of the expenses
will be reimbursed by the owner of the property.
Whether by passerby, act of nature, burglary, or any
other reason, I agree and I can, will, and should be
evicted if the broken window in question is not
repaired within twenty-four hours of being broken.

_____   _____
Landlord Signature   Tenant Signature

_____   _____
Date   Date

majority of judges are, you've got a legal document with your Tenants' signatures on it that says they are responsible for all broken windows. You didn't hold a gun to their heads when they signed it, so as badly as a pro-Tenant judge may want to rule in the Tenants' favor, he can't!

I have put together the greatest, bulletproof Landlord lease ever written. If you're interested, you can check it out at www.bulletprooflease.com. You will not find a better lease out there! You will understand it, the judge will understand it, and even the Tenants will understand it. What will they understand,

you ask? If the Tenants don't abide by the rules, they're gone. If they break something, they're held accountable. If they clog the toilet, they're responsible for the repairs. If they lock themselves out, they're liable for the locksmith's bill. If . . . You get the point. My bulletproof lease makes the Tenants responsible for all of their actions.

A great lease is an important tool
in the Landlording business.

TIP 2

Take Photographs before Move-in Day

Here is a little tip that can go a long way—in the courtroom, that is! I love this tip and if you use only one of the ideas in this book, I sure hope it's this one. It has saved my rear-end on numerous occasions.

I used to hate it when I had to go to court to evict a Tenant. I still do, but now I'm a lot more prepared. Why judges tend to think that Landlords are responsible for houses that Tenants demolish is beyond me. Half the time, I don't know who I want to beat over the head with the judge's gavel more—the Tenant or the judge!

It used to always be the same story. The Tenant would get behind on the rent, and then he or she would make up stories that the Landlord—me—wasn't fixing anything. The Tenant would then proceed into court with pictures of the damaged property. The judge would look at the pictures in awe, and then would look at me like I was a slumlord!

Finally, while sitting in court one day, a light bulb went off in my head. I thought to myself, "Mike, you moron! Why don't *you* take pictures of the property before the Tenant moves in? If you have pictures of how nice the property looked before the Tenant moved in, you will have proof that the only person who could have wrecked it or broke anything is the Tenant."

Here is how it works. Once you've finished all the work on a property, take a nice picture of each and every room in the home. Then on move in day, while you're walking your Tenants through it, have them sign the back of all of the pictures! So, for example, when you walk them into the master bedroom, show them the picture of that room and have them sign it. When you take them into the bathroom, show them the picture and have them sign it. When you show them the kitchen . . . you get the picture?!

Additionally, so there is no mix up later on, I put it into my lease that the Tenants agree that the pictures they are signing show the exact condition of the rooms that they are standing in. Then, I also tell the Tenants that the condition of the house when they signed the pictures and moved in, is the condition I expect it to be kept in.

These signed pictures will not only give you proof that the house was in excellent condition when the Tenant took possession of it, but they will also keep the Tenant from bringing his or her own pictures to court. Think about it. If you show a judge a signed picture of a room in excellent condition and the Tenant is dumb

Photographs ready to be signed by Tenants.

enough to show a picture of the same room in shambles, your case would only be strengthened!

As an added bonus, this tip also seems to deter most Tenants from inflicting damage to my properties in the first place. After I started incorporating the "Picture Tip" into my leases, the damage to my properties dropped dramatically! Give this tip a shot and you, too, will see less and less damage, and you won't have to fear the courtroom, either.

TIP 3

Video Record
the Entire Property

Okay, you're probably wondering why you should video record the property before the Tenant moves in if you already have signed pictures of it. Maybe I've been watching too many episodes of CSI, but there is no such thing as too much evidence. If you follow my advice, the judge can not only look at pictures when you go to court, but he or she can also see a video of the property and easily decide that you are not a slumlord—your Tenants are "slumtenants!"

Furthermore, taking a video of the property lets your Tenants know that you are not playing games with them, and that you are very serious about keeping your property in excellent condition. By going this extra mile, you're planting a seed in the Tenants' minds that you are not a Landlord who is going to tolerate any nonsense.

To avoid disputes about the accuracy of the footage down the road, I enter into my leases that Tenants are welcome to see the video footage of the property before they move in. However, I will not show it to them after they take possession of the property. The reason for this is that if they have been in the property for a year and then all of a sudden want to see the video footage, they're probably up to something. And chances are, it's not good!

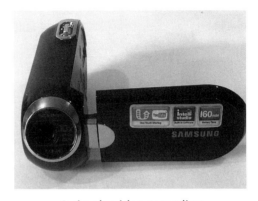

A simple video recording
could save you in court.

YOUR
BUSINESS

TIP 4

Consolidate Loans
into a Blanket Mortgage

Landlording can be an expensive business to break into. Luckily, blanket mortgages can help. What exactly are blanket mortgages? Can they really save you money? Do all banks have them? Many people have several questions when it comes to blanket mortgages, so let's start from the beginning.

Let's say that you have been purchasing properties for two years now. You bought six properties each year, so you now have twelve properties. Now let's say that you have three mortgage loans with two different banks, and two mortgage loans with three other banks—for a total of twelve separate loans with five different banks. The reason that so many banks are involved is that most will only give you three to four loans at a maximum. Then, you have to search for another bank that may give you two or three loans, and so on. This results in several different banks and several different loans, which can get confusing!

An easier way to keep better track of your money and payments is to consolidate all of your mortgages into one. This is called a *blanket mortgage*. If you are like me and like to stay organized with your finances, it's the best way to go. But staying organized isn't the only benefit!

When you take a blanket mortgage from a bank, that bank actually pays off all your other existing loans. The result is that you can now go back to those other banks and try to open a credit line, or, once again, use them for two or three mortgages in the future. Since you now have their trust because you paid them in full, they will more than likely be happy to do business with you again. Also, since a couple of banks have been paid off, your credit scores will begin to rise through the roof, giving you leverage when negotiating your next deal.

Now that you know what a blanket mortgage is and some of its benefits, it's time to discuss how, exactly, it can save you money. Continuing with our example, let's say that the twelve individual mortgage loans that you are going to be consolidating into a blanket mortgage each have an $80,000 balance. That adds up to a total of $960,000. The next step is to find your average interest rate. It's easy. Simply add up the interest rates for all twelve of your existing loans, and then divide by twelve. Here is an example:

Loan	Interest Rate
1	8.0 percent
2	9.0 percent
3	8.5 percent
4	7.5 percent
5	7.0 percent
6	9.0 percent
7	9.0 percent
8	8.0 percent
9	7.0 percent
10	7.0 percent
11	7.0 percent
12	8.0 percent
	95.0 (total of all interest)

95.0 divided by 12 = **7.91 percent average interest rate**

In this example, your average interest rate is 7.91 percent. Armed with this information, try to cut 1.5 percent off of that rate when you sit down to negotiate your blanket mortgage with the banker. In other words, ask for a 6.41 percent interest rate on your blanket mortgage. The reason you can ask for such a big reduction is because of the size and amount of the deal. A bank might have to do five or six separate loans to equal the amount of the single loan you are handing them. Also, the collateral is more than sufficient, considering you are throwing twelve homes into the mix.

When doing a loan like this, bankers can be pretty creative—they may be able to save you money on things like appraisals and document preparation fees, which they usually knock down quite a bit to get such a sizable loan to go through. You should also be able to get them down in interest rates and points, which are fees you pay to the bank to borrow money. One point is one percent of the borrowed amount. So if you take a $100,000 loan, one point would equal $1,000. The bottom line is that the bigger the loan is going to be, the sharper the bankers' pencils will get.

The one "catch," if you can call it that, is that not all banks do blanket mortgages, and here is why. If you have five properties that you would like to take loans on, most banks would rather you take five *different* loans. Why? The reason is simple—fees! They would rather charge you document preparation fees, wiring fees, credit check fees, and more, five times instead of just one, as would be the case with a blanket mortgage. If you plan on keeping your properties for the life of the loan, though, take the time to find a bank that offers blanket mortgages. They are simply the best way to go.

TIP 5
Stay Organized

Throughout this book, I have told you that certain things save time and money, both of which are very valuable things that you can never have enough of. In my mind, wasting time by being disorganized is the worst mistake one can make! Even Ben Franklin once said, "Lost time is never found again."

Everybody is given the exact same amount of time each day—twenty-four hours. How you use your time will determine if you are home and eating dinner with your family by four o'clock, or if you're sitting in rush hour traffic at five o'clock, complaining and wishing that you could have been home an hour earlier. Here are a few inexpensive ways to keep some valuable things organized, which will save you some time and get you home earlier each day:

The organized keyboard in my office.

Keys

Keep the keys to your properties on a tag and hang them on a key-board. That way, you'll never have to go searching for keys when you need to get into one of your properties. Don't be that Landlord that has to dig through a shoebox with fifty-five sets of keys in it just to find the one that you're looking for. Instead, have them neatly hung on a hook where they're easy to find!

Files

Keep a file of each and every property that you own. Make sure you keep them neatly arranged in alphabetical or numerical order in a filing cabinet—not in a box or a desk drawer. Then, simply place any important documents, such as a Hud-1 or insurance binder, directly into their dedicated files. This should keep things in very good order. Life is as easy as you make it!

The huge filing cabinet that I use.   Documents are placed into folders.

Hooks

Get things off of the floor and out of boxes by hanging them up! I can never see what's at the bottom of a box, so I'm a big believer in keeping stuff out in the open, right in front of me. That way, I know if it's not there that it's either missing, or that I'm out of it. Utilize empty space in your shop or in your basement by installing hooks. It will make your life a hell of a lot easier and it's cheap to do!

Extension cords neatly hung up in my shop.

A pegboard holding hardware supplies.

To motivate you and for your enjoyment, here are ten famous quotes on time and organization:

"We must use time as a tool, not a crutch."
—JOHN F. KENNEDY

"Time is what we want most, but we use worst."
—WILLIAM PENN

*"Until you value yourself, you won't value your time.
Until you value your time, you will do nothing with it."*
—M. SCOTT PECK

"You may delay, but time will not."
—BEN FRANKLIN

*"Much may be done in those little shreds and patches of time
which everyday produces, and which most men throw away."*
—CHARLES COLTON

"Day (noun). A period of twenty-four hours, mostly misspent."
—AMBROSE BIERCE

*"Organizing is something you do before you do something,
so that when you do it, it's not all mixed up."*
—A.A. MILNE

*"To be powerful you must be strong, and to have dominion
you must have a genius for organizing."*
—JOHN NEWMAN

"Science is organized knowledge. Wisdom is organized life."
—IMMANUEL KANT

"Don't agonize. Organize!"
—FLORENCE KENNEDY

TIP 6

Keep Showing Your Property

This tip will help you get your property rented as quickly as possible. If a prospective Tenant tells you that he or she likes your property but wants to look at a couple of others before making a decision, keep showing your property to other people. Do not consider it rented until you have a security deposit and a completed rental application in your hand.

Continuing to show your property creates a win-win situation for you. Either the first Tenant calls you back and decides to rent it before you have found someone else, or you find someone else. If the latter occurs, when the first Tenant calls back you can simply say the property has already been rented. It's like a sign I once saw in a car dealership. It read, "The car you said you would come back for tomorrow is the car that somebody else came back for today!"

TIP 7

Remain Confident

Never get discouraged when it comes to Landlording! You will have bad days and make mistakes in this business just like you would in any other, but every problem that you will run into has a solution. Trust me. Whether you find the answers to your problems in this book or you think a little on your own end, you will eventually figure everything out.

Furthermore, do your best to remain positive and to not let your mistakes get you down. The more motivated you stay, the further you will go. So, always think of your mistakes as constructive, future investments, because now that they've happened once, you know they're never gonna happen again!

Although problems will always annoy me, they no longer make me want to throw in the towel. Instead, they just make me think a little, and there's nothing wrong with thinking. Anyone can throw their hands up in the air and say, "I quit," but it's the people who rise up to challenges instead of running away from them that will be there in the end to reap the rewards!

DEALING WITH TENANTS

TIP 8

Do Not Give Your Personal Phone Numbers to Tenants

Unless you are looking for the fastest way to get committed into a mental hospital, don't give out your cell or home phone number to any Tenant under any circumstances. My first six Tenants received my home and cell phone numbers. Not long after, I had them changed! I now give Tenants only the number to my secondary office, which is hooked up to an answering machine, and I am much happier for it. Even if you don't have an office, per say, get a second phone line with a different number hooked up in your basement. Otherwise, you won't get any peace.

Trust me when I say that your Tenants will not only call you at eleven o'clock at night to tell you that the kitchen light blew out, but they'll also call you at four o'clock in the morning to tell you that it came back on. Whatever the case, let your Tenants talk to your answering machine. That way you can decipher what is important and what is not. To them, a creaking floorboard is an urgent situation. But you and your answering machine will be the judge of that! As a Landlord, you've got twenty-four hours to get to a true emergency repair. Anything else, well, you'll get to it as soon as possible.

Additionally, if you give your Tenants your personal phone numbers they will think that you're at their beck and call, which you're not! And not only should you expect your Tenants to call you, you should be prepared for their friends and family members who aren't even named on the lease to call you multiple times about problems, as well. For this reason, I learned to state in my leases that I will have phone conversations only with people named on the lease. I have the Tenants sign a separate form stating the same thing, as well, just to make sure they understand. Then, if a Tenant's boyfriend or mother ever calls you, you can move for eviction because he or she is violating the lease.

At this point you may be thinking that all of this sounds great, but you are still worried about what will happen in true emergency situations—namely fires and floods. Well, if a fire is ripping through one of my properties, I would hope my Tenants have enough common sense to call 9-1-1, not L-A-N-D-L-O-R-D! As far as floods go, I teach Tenants what to do in the event of a flood before they take possession of my properties. I walk them down to the basement and show them where and how to cut off the main water supply. I also include in my leases that they are to turn off the water before calling me. If they don't, my lease holds them fully responsible for all of the damages that the flood caused. These safeguards make it unnecessary for me to give Tenants my personal phone numbers, even for emergencies.

Get a second phone line and let an answering
machine screen calls from your Tenants.

TIP 9

Just Say No

This tip won't cost you a cent, but I guarantee that it will save you a ton of cash if you follow it correctly. It will also make you feel great. And all you have to do is just say, "No!"

When I first started out in this business I was a nice guy. Unfortunately, "nice guy" sounded more like "sucker" to some of my Tenants. Just how long after discovering this trait of mine did they begin trying to take advantage of me? Well, let's just say most of the time we weren't even through the front door yet!

The Tenants would cooperate and pay all of the money they owed upfront, until it was time for them to break balls . . . err, I mean, move in. As soon as we would reach the front door on move-in day, the B.S. would start. They would ask, "Are you going to put a screen door on here?" To which I would reply, "There wasn't a screen door on here when you first looked at the property, so why would you think I'd install one now?" They would always respond with some line of nonsense, like, "Because flies can get in," or "So my kids don't get out."

Anyway, for some reason I would say, "Maybe if you continue to pay your rent on time, I'll see about getting you a screen door." Then I'd open the front door and the B.S. would continue. As the Tenants continued through the house they would ask, "Are you going to put a doorbell on here?" "Are you going to put carpet down in here?" "Are you going to add some more outlets in here?" Are you gonna, are you gonna, are you gonna?!

Then, about a month would go by and after they had paid their first month's rent, whether it was on time or not, they would call and say, "I paid the rent, where's my screen door?" It didn't take me long to figure out that this was a test. Right from the beginning the Tenants will test you and see if you'll give into their demands. If you give into their first one, it'll all be downhill from there. It'll never end!

So, save yourself the headache and just say no from the beginning. No to every extra they want, and no to the infamous question, "Can I ask you a question?" After all, when you finished renovating your property, that's exactly what you did—finished! If it was good enough for you, then it's going to be good enough for them.

Here is a line that I like to use: "I did everything that I had to do to the property and I won't be doing anything else." Once your Tenants see that you're not willing to give in to them, they'll stop asking questions. Be straightforward. Don't beat around the bush and give them any misconceptions like, "I'll have to talk to my partner about getting you some carpet." If your Tenants see a chink in your armor, they won't quit until they get through it. The answer to their demands should always be, "No." Remember, you got into this business to make money, not friends!

TIP 10

Don't Spoil Good Tenants

I've had a lot of good relationships with Tenants who have respect-ed my properties, and that's the way it should be! I give them a nice place to live; they pay the rent on time and take care of the place. Unfortunately, these "good" Tenants tend to come with a catch. They often think that they deserve extras. By now, however, you know me well enough to know that I don't give into them, and nei-ther should you!

I've seen too many Landlords bend over backwards to keep their good Tenants happy. Sure you might be motivated to get to good Tenants' houses a little quicker for repairs, but what you can't do is go out of your way for them. Why? Let me tell you.

Let's say that you have some Tenants who have been living in one of your properties for two years. During that time, they've always kept it spotless and paid the rent on time. Then, one day one of them calls you up with a question that might go something like this: "Mike, you know I have been taking care of your property since I moved in, right?" "Correct," I would answer. "Well, since I'm a good Tenant of yours, I would like to get some new carpet in here. Could you replace it?"

Now, let's say the carpet for the living room, dining room, and hallway will run you $1,200. What are you supposed to do? I keep my own house clean but I don't see the mortgage company at my door with any prizes or rewards. . . .

Think of it this way. If you walked into your property and the Tenant had done $1,200 worth of damage, would you be irate? Of course you would! You would have to spend $1,200 of your money to fix the problem. So, what's the difference if you're spending your money to give your Tenant carpet or if you're spending it on repairs?

There is no difference! It is still your money that you are spending! New carpet won't do anything for you other than make your Tenant happy. It's a cosmetic repair and it doesn't have to be done.

The bottom line is this. If a repair or upgrade to the property benefits you—items such as a roof, a heater, a water heater, etc.— then you're spending your money in the right place. If, on the other hand, a repair or upgrade to the property benefits your Tenant— items such as carpet, paint, screen doors, etc.—then you're wasting your money. A fool and his money will soon be parted, so don't be a fool!

When your property looks as good as this, don't
make unnecessary cosmetic repairs—even for good Tenants.

TIP 11

Don't Stress
about Tenant Cleanliness

This is a simple tip, but it will give you peace of mind. Do to not let yourself become preoccupied by the cleanliness—or lack thereof—of your Tenants. Tenant cleanliness is one of the things that aggravated me to no end when I first became a Landlord. I'd give a Tenant a nice, clean property to live in, and sometimes it would be filthy within a month! What might help you sleep a little better at night is knowing that it happens to every Landlord at least once—it's not just you!

When I first got started in this business and owned less than ten homes, I would get so mad when I would go into one of them and see that it was a pig-pen—dishes stacked two-feet high in the sink, laundry all over the house, stains on the carpets; the list goes on and on. I would snap at the Tenants and tell them that they had twenty-four hours to clean up the joint or I would evict them.

For those twenty-four hours my stomach would burn, I would be in a bad mood, and I wouldn't be able to sleep. When I would return to inspect the "clean up" of the property the next day, I would only get angrier! The Tenants would always do a terrible job of straightening up the place. They would jam junk in the closet, run the vacuum, spray some air freshener, light some incense, take out the trash, and call it a day. Just enough to shut me up I suppose. Then, ten to one odds the house would look the way it did the day before within a half an hour of my leaving!

Once I owned more than ten homes, I finally got it through my thick head that this is a business. If I kept staying up at night worrying about which Tenants were taking out the trash and doing the dishes, I wasn't gonna make it in this line of work. There were much more important things that I needed to be worrying about instead, like getting paid, purchasing more properties, getting them rented, and building my own empire!

My point with all of this is to simply not let yourself stress out about Tenants' cleanliness. I now look back and laugh about the things that used to anger me. Why the hell was I worried and mad about dirty dishes in a sink I never saw? Whether the dishes were there or not, I was still getting paid on the property every month. Nowadays, getting paid is the number one thing that I worry about, and believe me, my worries are much fewer and farther between.

SAFETY, SAFETY, SAFETY

TIP 12

Keep the Doors Locked

When I drive by a house that is being rehabbed, I'm always amazed when I see that the contractors working on it have left the front door and windows wide open, the radio blaring, and saw horses, wood, and tools unattended out front. Where are the workers? Who knows! But wherever they are, they're not out front with the materials, which can and will walk away if they're not being watched. I don't know about you, but I work too hard to have my tools ripped off.

I've also heard stories of thieves actually walking *into* houses and taking off with screw guns, saws, and other tools. Where were the workers? Perhaps they were on the roof, in the basement, or maybe around the corner getting a soda at the store. Regardless, they weren't watching the supplies like they should have been and they didn't have the doors locked. In fact, they probably wouldn't even notice or catch a thief unless he unplugged the radio, because that's only thing they would miss anyway! (Yes, the radio bit is a jab at my workers.)

I'm going to add one more thing about keeping your doors locked. Not only does doing so keep thieves out, but it also prevents city and building inspectors from entering! If an inspector is driving down the street and sees extension cords running out of the front door and plywood being cut on the front lawn, he may stop in to see if you have permits for the work that is being performed. Even though you don't need a permit for cosmetic repairs, if the inspector gets into your property he will go out of his way to find something to hang you on. Had the front door been closed and locked, he never would have stopped. Lock the doors and cut the wood in the basement!

TIP 13
Don't Open the Door

Here is a quick tip that might very well save your life. If you hear somebody knocking on the front door of your property while you're inside working, do not open it under any circumstances! I know a contractor who did and he was greeted with a brick to the face. It turns out that he had apparently parked his van a little too close to the neighbor's BMW.

If someone is knocking at the front door, go upstairs, open the window that overlooks it, and yell down, "Can I help you?" That way, you will be able to see who is at the door, figure out what they want, see if there is anything in their hands, and most importantly, turn them away if you need to! Think about it. If you are working on a property that you just purchased and you don't know anybody in the neighborhood, who is going to come visit you? Trouble, that's who! I'm not trying to scare you, but sometimes bad things can happen if you are not prepared. It's always better to be safe than sorry.

You never know who's going to be on the other side.

TIP 14

Deny Being the Landlord

When you are getting your property ready to be rented, a lot of passersby will be very nosy. They will want to know all about your intentions for the home—whether you are going to be selling it, living in it, or renting it out. The answer to the questions, "Are you the Landlord?" and "Are you going to be renting the house?" should always be, "I don't know what the guy is going to be doing with it. I'm just a contractor. I can give you his phone number if you like."

By answering these questions in this form, you are doing yourself two favors. First, you're leaving the door open if the passersby really did want to rent the property. If they make the effort to follow-up and call, they are probably serious about renting—not just wasting your time walking through it and possibly casing the place to see what they can come back and steal.

Second, you're preventing them from thinking that you are the Landlord or owner of the property. When some people hear you're the Landlord, they'll automatically think you're rich. That may be the case, but you don't want the whole neighborhood knowing it because it will increase your chances of getting mugged. Keep your mouth shut, tell them nothing, and complete your project. "He who speaks much is much mistaken." I got that quote out of a fortune cookie!

TIP 15

Always have Someone Foot Your Ladder

I occasionally run into a Landlord that I talk to at the Section 8 office. While we wait to get our leases signed, we talk about this, that, and the other, and we have become pretty good friends just through running into each other so much. Well, one day he hobbled into the office with a cast on his leg that went up to his thigh. So, I of course asked him what happened. Here is what he told me.

"Mike, you're not gonna believe this one. I was capping a window from a twenty-foot ladder and this guy comes walking up to the bottom of it. He told me to throw down my money or he was going to yank the ladder down with me on it! I told him that I didn't have any cash on me and he said, 'Then drop down your screw gun.' I dropped it down to him, but he still knocked the ladder out from underneath me."

My buddy ended up with a broken heel, fibula, and tibia. He was in a cast for four months and he still walks with a limp.

The lesson here is one of prevention. Always have somebody foot your ladder. I'm not a big fan of heights, so I always have someone at the bottom of my ladder anyhow. But even if heights weren't a fear of mine, you can be sure I'd have someone bracing the bottom of my ladder after that story! By doing so, you're staying safe in two ways. One, the ladder cannot accidentally slide out from under you. And two, no one can intentionally kick it out from under you.

TIP 16
Know Who You are Hiring

I used to hire a guy to do concrete work on some of my properties. He owned a couple of properties of his own, as well. Anyway, he was in the process of cleaning one out one day, when he made a near fatal mistake. A guy walked up to him off the street and asked if he needed a hand. They both quickly agreed to an eight dollar per hour starting rate and the guy began helping with the clean out.

By lunchtime, the guy had put in three hours and asked if he could get a ten dollar advance out of his pay so he could get some lunch. The Landlord agreed and like a fool, opened his wallet and gave the guy the ten bucks. The guy returned after lunch and went back to work. Within fifteen minutes, he snuck up behind the Landlord and cracked him over the head with an aluminum base-ball bat that had been in the property—not once, not twice, but seven times! He not only wanted to rob him, he wanted to kill him.

Again, the lesson here is prevention. Never, ever hire a guy off the street that you don't know. Even when I hire someone to sim-ply cut a couple of lawns, I learn his name, where he lives, and whether he has a criminal background. You'll be surprised at what entering a name or social security number into an Internet search engine can tell you. Another helpful investigative website is www.phonebust.com. For a small fee, they'll provide you with a wealth of information on the individual in question.

Also, I don't think I have to tell you this but just in case, never pull out your wallet or any form of money in front of a total stranger. To you, fifty bucks might not be a lot, but to a drug addict, it's a fortune. Neither you or I need our heads split open, nor do we need a guy coming back later to rip the copper out of our houses. Do some investigative work upfront and save yourself the headache—quite literally—later.

TIP 17
Perform a
Background Check

The same investigative research you perform on the workers you hire should also be done on your potential Tenants. Making sure they aren't criminals is your number one priority. But with Tenants, it's also important to make sure they won't destroy your property after they move in, so some additional checks are necessary.

For some reason, a supplementary background check that several Landlords like wasting their time with is calling the Tenant's present Landlord. Forget it! This process usually works in reverse, and let me explain why. If a Landlord called me and wanted information about a bad Tenant of mine, I would tell him that he or she is the greatest Tenant in the world! Why? Because little would the inquiring Landlord know that he would be adopting an awful Tenant of mine, thereby relieving me of a burden.

On the other hand, if a Landlord called me and asked about a good Tenant of mine, I would be hesitant to give him good information. The reason is simple. I wouldn't want to lose a good Tenant. So as you can see, it's a waste of time to call other Landlords. You won't know if you are getting truth or lies!

Instead, use this trick to perform a spontaneous background check of your own. After you agree to rent your property to prospective Tenants, get their phone number and the address of the property they are currently occupying. Tell them you'll call when the lease is ready to be signed so you can meet up somewhere to do it. However, keep it to yourself that your *real* plan is to simply show up at their door without warning. When you do, you will have the lease in hand and tell them that you were in the neighborhood so you thought you'd save them a trip.

Before they actually sign the lease, tell them the last thing you need to do to qualify them is to take a quick look through their current residence. If they deny you access and won't let you see the inside, don't rent to them because they're obviously hiding something—bad housekeeping, damages, a pet, illegal Tenants, or whatever the case may be. If they're wrecking the place they're in now, yours is next. If, however, their current home is not too bad and you don't see a lot of damages, then rent them your property. Don't get too carried away and break out the white gloves for inspection. If you do, you'll never get your house rent-ed. Strictly look for heavy damages that could cost heavy cash to fix.

Finally, if the Tenants ask you to come back to-morrow instead of inviting you in right then, don't! What they're really asking for is time to clean up the place and get rid of every-thing they are hiding, such as a pet. You either get in that day or you don't rent to them.

Performing a spontaneous background check.

TIP 18
Never Use a
"For Rent" Sign

You might think that anywhere and everywhere would be a good place to advertise that your home is for rent. In your mind, more exposure increases the likelihood that you will rent your property quickly. However, you may be placing your property in danger! By advertising your unoccupied home, you may be giving thieves a map right to its front door. What's their treasure? Anything they can get their hands on if they get in—copper, carpets, light fixtures, heaters, stoves, and more.

Now that you're aware of this, you probably want to know how to prevent break-ins and thefts from happening. It's simple. Never hang a "For Rent" sign in the window of your rental! Not only does such a sign advertise that your property is for rent, it advertises that it is vacant. On the back of the sign you may as well write, "Thieves, after you're done ripping me off, could you please lock the door behind you?"

As the saying goes, "Locks only keep the honest people out." If crooks know that no one is living in the property and they want to get in, believe me, they will get in. Hell, they might even stay a night or two! So forget about using "For Rent" signs. The only thing they accomplish is to alert thieves that no one is in the property to stop a break in.

Instead, run an ad in the local paper to get your property rented, but don't give the full address. For instance, your ad might read something like this: "Three bedroom home for rent. 25xx block of Hobson Street. $760 per month, plus utilities." You'd then give your phone number. That way, you have control over who hears the address and who doesn't.

Never use a "For Rent" sign like this one.

TIP 19

Never Hold
an Open House

When trying to get your property rented, never hold an open house! An open house is when you call all the people who are interested in renting your property and tell them to come view it on the same day at the same time. You will most likely get your house rented, but you will also probably have to break up two or three fights in the process. If there is more than one person who would like to rent your property, be prepared for one of them to say that they saw it first or that they called you first. You might as well wear a referee shirt! And furthermore, even if the potential renters don't fight amongst themselves, once you make a decision, the people that you don't choose may want to fight you!

Here is how to prevent that scenario from playing out. Simply space your showings a half an hour apart. Create a list of names and phone numbers of who is coming when, and bring it with you so you can stay organized. Then, let's say the second person to look at the home wants to rent it and has the necessary security deposit. Fill out all the necessary forms—if they are on Section 8 it will be a Section 8 packet; if they are not on Section 8 it will be a rental application and credit check form—and then call the other people on your list to cancel. Tell them you will keep their numbers and if any of your other properties open up, you will call them back to take a look. If they start fighting with you over the phone, at least this way you can hang up and cross them off of your list for good!

INTERIOR WORK

TIP 20

Quickly and Efficiently
Clean Out Your Property

A lot of times in this business, you buy a property "as is"—meaning you buy it with the understanding that you're getting it in its current condition. The way it looked when you made your offer is the way it is going to look when you make your settlement. In some cases, an elderly person has died and all their belongings remain in the property. In other cases, a bank has foreclosed on a property and the family that was living there takes their valuable possessions and leaves behind their trash and junk. Regardless, that is how you will be taking possession of the property, and you will undoubtedly need to clean it out.

Before starting the clean-out, make a list of everything that you want to eliminate. Take a walk through the property and make decisions about which items are staying and which are going. Obviously you will be removing all the trash from the property, but there are many more objects in the home on which you'll have to make a decision, including carpets, vanities, sink bases, light fixtures, and more. The next several tips should help you in your decision making process. Some items could be expensive to replace in the beginning, but doing so may end up saving you money in the long run. Your clean-out will not be complete until each and every object that you wanted to eliminate is crossed off of your list.

There are two ways to remove rubbish from the home. Both are simple, but one is cheap and one is expensive. Let's get the expensive way covered first. Pick up the phone book and call three different "clean out" companies. You can find them under the recycling category in the phone book. Invite them out to the property, show them what you want removed from it, and get their price.

Hire the company that gives you the lowest offer, and then wait until the workers finish the job to pay them. I never pay until a job is complete. If the workers tell me they need two or three hundred dollars to get started, then they are not very good businessmen. Move on to the next guys who don't require a deposit. Once you pay, the clean-out job is done. But I guarantee that if you call someone out of the phone book, you're going to pay at least triple the amount it would cost you to do it yourself.

This brings us to the cheaper method, which is doing it yourself. If you own a pick-up truck it will make things a lot easier, but if you don't, you can still get the job done. If you have a truck, you will first need trash cans, and plenty of them. I recommend you use the Brute cans with handles on the side. They are carried by Home Depot, and I am sure if you look around you can find them at any major department store. Using trash cans is a more efficient and quicker way to get trash out of the house and into the truck than just using your hands. Simply pack the cans as full as you can get them and then drag or carry them out to the truck. Once you get about twelve cans—most six foot beds will hold ten cans and most eight foot beds will hold fourteen cans—start stacking them neatly and tightly onto the back of your truck.

When your truck is full, the next step is to figure out where you will be taking the trash. Once again, you will need your local yellow pages. Look up the words "recycling services" or "recycling centers." All of the places listed under those categories should accept trash and rubbish, and there should definitely be one within five miles of your home. Find the center that is closest to you and go there to dump your trash. Since you have already neatly placed your rubbish into trash cans, you will now save even more valuable time when dumping. Simply take the cans off the truck and dump them. Just think how much longer it would take you to unload the trash if you had just thrown it directly in the truck bed instead!

Heavy-duty
Brute trash cans.

Pick-up truck loaded with trash cans.

If you do not have a pick-up truck but still want to do the clean-out job yourself, get a dumpster delivered to your property. Once again, these companies can be found in the phone book under "recycling." The dumpsters come in various sizes and there is no time limit on how long you can have them—the company will charge you by size only. A ten yard dumpster is typically $350; a twenty yard dumpster is typically $490; a thirty yard dumpster is typically $620; and a forty yard dumpster is typically $780. Once you fill the dumpster, the company you got it from will come back out and remove it. This is not a bad way to go. However, sometimes the city will make you get a permit to place the dumpster in front of the house. Also, you may get complaints from the neighbors about the dumpster clogging up the parking on the street.

Cleaning out your property is a dirty job, but it must get done, and it must get done first. Start your project out on the right foot and do the clean-out properly. Make sure that everything you want to get rid of in the house is eliminated before you move on to the next step. If you purchase a home that is loaded with furniture and trash, the minute it's gone and you've swept the house you will notice a huge difference. You will actually see what you have to work with and what it will take to complete your project. Now is the time to go from room to room, wall to wall, and remove all the screws, nails, picture hooks, curtain rods, etc. that still remain. This is one less thing you will have to do before painting the unit.

Here's one final tip about clean-outs. If you are planning on purchasing and renting more than ten homes, you might consider buying a stake body truck. Used ones go for around $5,500, and they make clean-outs quick work. Simply pack the bed as full as you can get it, take it to the dump, remove the gates, hit the dump button, and you're done. I wouldn't recommend getting a stake body if you are just going to be purchasing a couple of homes, but if your intentions are larger, it may be a good investment.

TIP 21

Change All of
the Light Fixtures

After you clean out your property and begin to get it ready for renting, make sure you remove any and all light fixtures, including ceiling fans, chandeliers, fluorescent lights, and others. What are you going to be replacing them with? Nine dollar light fixtures from Home Depot!

Florescent lights are especially important to get rid of, and the reason why is simple: They're a pain in the neck! Tenants will always tell you that they don't know how to replace the bulbs, that they can't afford new bulbs, or that they don't know where to get new bulbs. They won't have this problem with the inexpensive Home Depot light fixtures, though. With them, all Tenants need to do is simply remove the globe, screw in the new, generic light bulb, and they're done.

In addition to florescent lights, I also eliminate chandeliers and ceiling fans. It doesn't matter if your ceiling fan is a Hampton Bay worth a hundred bucks—replace it! Again, the reason for this is simple. If you move Tenants into a property and it has an expensive ceiling fan or chandelier, they will expect you to replace it with a brand new, expensive ceiling fan or chandelier when it breaks. If, however, you have a nine dollar light fixture in place when the Tenants move in and it breaks, there won't be any arguments as to what you're replacing it with.

Furthermore, when you eliminate ceiling fans you also eliminate the risk of injury. Here is an exact email I received from a fellow Landlord after he had read my first book:

Mike, I received your book on Friday and read it twice over the weekend. I couldn't put the damn thing down (look, another

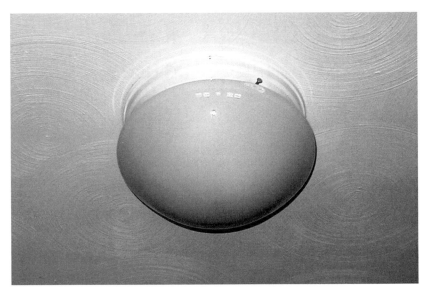

Nine dollar Home Depot light fixture.

Avoiding injuries is a great reason to remove ceiling fans like this one.

plug!!)! I loved every chapter but one, the "Elimination" chapter. Not that you weren't right on the money with everything that you told of eliminating, but I was so mad that I didn't order the book a year sooner. Here is what happened.

A ceiling fan was in the master bedroom of a house that I purchased. The thing was practically brand new so I left it. My Tenant moves in and for the first year she is there, everything is fine. Then I get a call from her lawyer asking me for the name of my insurance carrier. I asked him what happened and here is what he told me.

The Tenant had two sons, one twelve and one ten. They were jumping up and down on the bed to see who could touch the ceiling first. What they forgot to do was turn off the ceiling fan! The twelve-year-old got up high enough that one of the blades, which was going 60 mph, struck him in the face. Not only did it rip him open (14 stitches), it put out his left eye.

The case is still in court and although I have insurance, I can hardly wait to hear the outcome. My nerves are shot! When I was reading your book and came to the part of eliminating ceiling fans, I wanted to kick myself in the ass. If you can get this story passed along, I would appreciate it. I wouldn't want something as stupid as this coming back to haunt anyone else.

Victor Arroyo
Bronx, New York

Vic, I'll get the message out alright. People, are you starting to get the idea here? Elimination is a Landlord's best friend! Keep reading to find out what other items it will benefit you to eliminate.

TIP 22
Eliminate the Garbage Disposal

If your property does not have a garbage disposal in it, you're already in great shape. If it does, eliminate it immediately! I don't care if it's brand new, working properly, and cost a couple hundred bucks. Get rid of it unless you like headaches, because that's exactly what garbage disposals are. There are so many things that can go wrong with them that your Tenant will call you at least five times a year for garbage disposal problems alone. They clog up your sink, the blades get stuck, they cause injuries, the reset button pops off—the list goes on and on. You name it, it happens, and your Tenant calls.

If you leave the garbage disposal installed and something does happen, you'll rarely get an honest answer from your Tenants when you ask them what they threw down the sink. They will all say something along the lines of, "Nothing. I didn't throw anything down the sink." Then, when you start pulling bones and plastic forks out of the garbage disposal, your Tenants will turn into confused actors. A surprised look will come across their faces and they'll say, "I don't know how that got down there!" Well, I do! Instead of scraping their plates into the trash can, they scraped them into the sink because of the disposal.

It is in your best interest as a Landlord to eliminate problems before they become problems. And believe me, garbage disposals are nothing but problems. They can also cause injuries! Here is another email I received from a fellow Landlord after reading my first book:

> Mike, I just completed your book. I've been in this business for several years now and I must say there are things in there [the book] that I never would have thought of doing. Although you guys remove garbage disposals to eliminate clogs, I found

another reason to eliminate them. Unfortunately, I received your book a little too late!

On January 2, 2007, I received a call from a Tenant of mine. She informed me that her son was trying to release a plastic fork from the clogged garbage disposal. Well, he got the fork loose but he also lost the tips of three fingers! What he did was leave the switch in the "On" position while trying to free the fork. The instant the fork came loose, the blades began to chop.

Of course, I'm now being sued. I have insurance and my properties are set up in an LLC, but it is still one big hassle. I'm sure before it's said and done the kid will get paid and my insurance will go up. I just wanted to pass a story along to you and I hope it gets in your next book.

John Glasgow
St. Louis, Missouri

If those are not enough reasons for you to eliminate your garbage disposals, then I don't know what else to tell ya!

Eliminate garbage disposals like this one.

TIP 23

Choose Stoves Carefully

When you purchase a property and the stove works properly, simply clean it and leave it in place. However, if you have to replace it, make sure you choose what to install very carefully. There are two types of stoves—electric and gas. Never choose electric! Electric stoves are more expensive than gas stoves, they cost more to fix, and they'll cause you way more problems. Additionally, the two heating elements in electric stoves—bake and broil—never really seem to last long. Once they crack it's over, and the element has to be replaced.

I don't know why, but it seems like these stove-related problems always happen around Thanksgiving and Christmas. So now you have a Tenant calling you on Christmas Eve, hollering that she has fifty-five people coming over for Christmas dinner and nothing to cook it in. What a way to kick off your holiday! Stick with gas stoves and you'll rarely get calls like this.

Always install gas stoves.

When you buy a gas stove, you want to steer clear of those with electronic igniters. All four burners have one, and when they go bad—which happens quite often—they are very expensive to replace. Stick with the old-fashioned pilots. If they go out, they simply need to be re-lit with a match, which is much cheaper than a repairman bill!

TIP 24
Remove the Dishwasher

If you purchase a property that has a dishwasher, remove it! Dishwashers are a lot like garbage disposals in the sense that they are nothing but headaches. I haven't heard of many injuries caused by dishwashers—other than big dents in peoples' wallets—but they do cause several other problems. For example, dishwashers drain directly into the kitchen sink, often causing it to clog. And if they are not clogging the sink, the timer is going haywire or the pump is leaking or not draining. It's always something, and the minute this appliance stops working, you'll get a hundred phone calls from your irate Tenant!

Hey, I know that nobody likes to do dishes, including me. But save yourself the dishwasher headache in your rental property. Think about it. If the dishwasher in your own house stops working, you call the appliance man to come fix it. But if the dishwasher in your rental property stops working, your Tenant will call you. The only thing these scenarios have in common is that you will be paying for both. Eliminate the dishwasher before Tenants move in and they will never even miss it. Leave it and you will continue to pay—in more ways than one!

Eliminate dishwashers like this one.

TIP 25

Remove All
220-Volt Electrical Outlets

Get rid of all 220 lines, especially when the outlet falls under a window. The reason for this is so that your Tenant does not put an air conditioner in the window. It's not that I don't want my Tenants to feel comfortable in the summer; I just don't want them to install window-unit air conditioners. Sometimes, the air conditioners that the Tenants want to hook up are old, gigantic, and weigh about 200 pounds. All three of these factors go against you.

If the air conditioner is old, somehow, someway, it will end up blowing fuses like there is no tomorrow. And what happens when your Tenants blow a fuse? They call you.

If the air conditioner is gigantic, it may not fit into the window. But that does not mean your Tenant won't try to force it to fit. Usually, the glass in the window ends up cracking or breaking. And what happens when a window breaks? Your Tenants call you.

And finally, if by some miracle your Tenants get their 200-pound air conditioner into the window without breaking the glass, you still have another problem: You've got 200 pounds sitting on top of a vinyl window. Although the vinyl may be pretty strong, it's a good bet that it will be cracked or destroyed when the Tenants eventually take the air conditioner out of the window.

If all of that is still not enough to convince you, another reason you don't want an air conditioner in the window is because it presents the possibility of a lawsuit. Should an air conditioner fall from an upstairs window and hit someone or someone's car below, you know who that person is coming after—you! Or, to be more specific, your insurance carrier!

I'm not saying that removing a 220 outlet will work every time in your effort to keep Tenants from installing window-unit air conditioners, but most of the time it will. Not too many Tenants are going to pay an electrician a few hundred dollars or more to install a 220 line for them. They would rather ask you if you would get one installed. And after reading what you just read, I'm sure you won't hesitate to tell them no!

Removing electrical outlets will help you prevent
Tenants from installing air conditioners like this one.

TIP 26

Replace Wall-Mounted Sinks with Vanities

In this business, there are times when spending a little money in the beginning will save a lot of money in the long run. When dealing with bathroom sinks, this is always the case. If you have a wall-mounted sink, remove it and replace it with a vanity. Over the years, I have found that wall-mounted sinks can get ripped from the wall. Also, the trap is exposed with no protection surrounding it, almost begging to be broken. On the other hand, a vanity cannot get ripped off of the wall and the cabinet protects the trap from being damaged. Install a vanity before your Tenant moves in and you will prevent both of these future repairs!

Wall-mounted sink.

Bathroom vanity.

TIP 27

Stick to
Single-Handle Faucets

If you purchase a home that needs sink or tub faucets replaced, always replace them with a single-handle Moen faucet! The reason to choose single-handle faucets is because they will give you fewer headaches. They will cut down your chances of something leaking by 50 percent, since you only have one stem instead of two—a hot and a cold.

There are several brands of single-handle faucets, but in my experience, Moen is the best. They rarely leak, but if they do they are very easy to re-washer. Simply shut off the water, pull out the cartridge, change the rubber washers, pop the faucet back into place, and you're done! There is no need for a seat tool, because there will be no more rusted out or stripped seats. Can it get any easier?

Three-handle faucet.

Moen single-handle faucet.

TIP 28
Always Use Caulk

A tube of caulk only costs about two bucks and can prevent hundreds of dollars worth of repairs, yet a lot of Landlords don't even bother to use it! You should always caulk and re-caulk your tubs and sinks. Start by using a razor knife or scraper to remove the old, worn-out caulk. Then, put a nice thin bead of caulk along the edges of your tub or sink, press it neatly into the cracks with your finger, and you're done. This will not only give your tub and sink a nice, clean appearance, it will also prevent water from leaking behind the walls and down into the room that is underneath the bathroom!

Neatly caulked tub.

TIP 29

Hang Shower Curtains

As I'm sure you can tell by now, I'm not one for giving away a bunch of free stuff to my Tenants. However, the one free thing that I *do* give to every one of my Tenants is a shower curtain. Hell, I even hang it for them, because just leaving one in its package in the property as a "move in gift" does not guarantee that your Tenant will cooperate and hang it!

Believe me on this one, because I've seen preventable problems happen more than once. If you do not follow my advice and hang a shower curtain, your Tenants will call you as soon as two weeks after they move in saying there's a leak coming through their din-

ing room ceiling. You will then head over to the house and proceed upstairs to see where the water is coming from. And what do ya know? Your new, lazy Tenants never even bothered to hang the shower curtain! You now possibly have a damaged bathroom floor and you definitely have a damaged dining room ceiling. So, spend the extra ten bucks for a shower curtain and rod, make sure you hang it, and avoid this call!

Hang shower curtains
before Tenants move in.

TIP 30

If the Flooring is Okay, Leave it Alone

If your kitchen or bathroom floors are ceramic, don't touch 'em! Leave them alone because you're already in good shape. After all, why spend money if you don't have to? I've seen countless Landlords waste money by installing carpet, linoleum, or stick-down tile over top of perfectly good ceramic floors, just because they didn't like the color!

Ceramic tile is as solid as it gets, and it won't wear out, tear, or get destroyed by water. So, why put anything over top of it? Carpets will get filthy, linoleum will rip, and stick-down tiles will get destroyed by water. Simply leave the ceramic floor alone and save yourself some cash.

The same thing goes for linoleum and stick-down tile floors. Although they aren't quite as good as ceramic tiles, if they are in good shape, leave them alone. Remember, you aren't out here trying to win a beauty contest; you're out here trying to make and save a buck. If you start trying to replace things that are in good shape, you won't have any money left to replace the things that break!

Okay, with that being said, now let's say the floors in the kitchen and bathroom are cracked, ripped, or have missing tiles. Obviously, something must be done. The cheapest and easiest way to replace them is to use stick-down tiles. Although I won't say it is fun, anybody with half a brain can install them. Here's how to do it, step by step:

1. Go to a home-improvement store like Home Depot and purchase a product called luan. It is sold for about ten bucks a sheet. Then,

simply cover your entire existing floor with it, using underlayment nails to secure it. Make sure you use underlayment nails because they are ridged at the top and they will never work themselves out. Once they're in, they're in.

2. Go back to the store and buy stick-down tiles made by Images. They cost about a dollar a tile, and once the luan is down, they're super easy to install—simply peel and stick. I have tried using both cheaper and more expensive tiles, but I have found that the Images tiles work the best. The cheaper tile is too thin, doesn't stick as well, and wears out pretty quickly. And the more expensive tile is actually harder to work with. It's a little bit thicker, which slows you down because it's harder to cut, especially when it's cold. It will also wear out your razorblade a lot quicker—not that the blades are that expensive to begin with, but if you have to stop every ten minutes to change them out you can see where this would get rather time-consuming.

3. When you are finished sticking down the tiles, nail a carpet bar over the edge of the door opening. This will prevent the tiles from popping up. After you've done that, you're finished and your floor looks great!

I've used linoleum instead of stick-down tiles in the past, and although it goes down faster because it is only one piece, you're screwed when it rips. The reason I say *when* it rips, is because it always does. Most of the time, the damage-doing culprit is the bottom of a kitchen table or a chair leg. The rip starts small, but then it gets bigger and bigger, and the next thing you know you're replacing the entire floor again. That is what I love about stick-down tiles. If one or two of them get a hole, you only need to peel up and replace the damaged tiles, not the whole floor!

Porch floor before tile.   Porch floor after tile.

Stick-down tiled kitchen floor.

TIP 31

Think Long and Hard
Before Installing Carpet

I'll get right to the point: I hate spending money on carpeting! I can't think of a bigger waste of money than installing carpets in a rental property. I used to do it, and sometimes they didn't even last five years. It's not that I was putting down cheap carpet as thin as Christmas wrapping paper, either. The stuff I was installing was twenty-year carpet at ten dollars per yard. It might have lasted twenty years in my house or yours, but I was lucky to get five years out of it in a rental property. To illustrate my point, let me give you a David Letterman-style top ten list of reasons why I hate installing carpets:

10. "Mom, I spilled my glass of Hawaiian Punch all over the living room carpet." "Don't worry about it baby, it's not ours, it's the Landlord's."

9. Do you really think the no eating or drinking in the living room rule is going to be enforced?

8. The "Please Remove Your Shoes" sign ain't gonna be read!

7. Here's a hint for the number of times they will have the carpet cleaners over to the house: It comes before one.

6. You can evict the Tenants, but if they sneak a pet into your property you won't be evicting the fleas or the cat urine smell anytime soon.

5. Some of the people you rent to don't own a vacuum.

4. You won't be lying on the carpets or running your toes through them, but you will be paying to replace them.

3. If the Tenants decide to paint anything, the carpets will become their drop cloths.

2. Carpeting is an expensive investment for possibly only a five-year return.

1. There are cheaper and better ways to make floors look good and stay looking good!

For the above-mentioned reasons and more, I will only replace the carpets in a rental house if it is the last resort. If water has buckled the floorboards or the flooring underneath the carpet looks like a jig-saw puzzle, then there is no other choice. But consider your options first. If the carpets that were down when you purchased the property aren't half bad, leave them. If, however, they are destroyed beyond cleaning or repair—stained, ripped, pet odor, the whole nine yards—remove them and take a look at what's underneath.

If it's an older home, about 99 percent of the time you'll find hardwood flooring, and about 80 percent of those times the hardwoods will be in good or excellent shape. If you can get away with mopping and throwing some hardwood floor wax on them, great! If they look like they are pretty hammered with scratches and are fading, though, have them restored. It's still cheaper than installing carpet.

My hardwood floor guy will come out to the home and sand and varnish every room in a three-bedroom house for $600; it's usually $100 more for each additional bedroom. Then, so what if Tenants don't take off their shoes, spill soda on the floor, or eat in the living room? A little dirt and a spill or two aren't going to ruin hardwoods. That's what's great about them. They may not look as good as carpets or be as comfortable, but they will save you cash!

Another thing I started doing was painting floors. If a house had good carpets or flooring throughout, aside from, let's say, the master bedroom, I would paint the floor with Rust-Oleum gray, oil-based paint; or as I like to call it, "carpet in a can." If you want your carpet in a can to give you a high pile, just give the floor two coats (Joke!). Your floor will look like that of a Navy battleship when you've finished painting it, but it will look clean and you'll save some cash. I've done this trick in a pinch about fifty times and I've never had any Tenants' complain about it.

Here is another thing to chew on—carpets can lead to lawsuits! That's right, if a Tenant falls down a flight of stairs, for example, the first thing he or she is going to say is that the carpet was loose and created a tripping hazard. If it can be proved, you're liable.

And finally, not only do these tips prevent the Tenants from suing you and dirtying the carpets, they totally eliminate any chance of the Tenants calling you and asking you to come clean the carpets that they dirtied!

Excellent hardwoods under carpet.

Restored hardwood floor.

TIP 32

Replace Outlets and Switches

I have my electrician replace every outlet, switch, toggle plate, ground fault interrupter (GFI), and light fixture in each and every house I purchase before my Tenants move in. This is because most electrical problems have to do with old, faulty outlets and switches. So, by changing them to new ones, you eliminate a ton of potential problems.

At most home-improvement stores, the outlets and switches go for about fifty cents a piece, the GFIs go for about eleven dollars, and the light fixtures go for about nine dollars. Add up all of the materials for an average rental house and the total will come out to about $125, which is a great investment considering you'll never get a call for electrical problems. Quite a deal, right?!

If that's not enough to convince you, consider this. By replacing outlets and switches, you are also eliminating the chance of an electrical fire, which could cause thousands of dollars in damages. Do yourself a favor and get the electrical upgrades done before you rent your property!

Replace all outlets, switches, and GFIs.

TIP 33

Use Thick Sleeves to Paint

This tip may seem like common sense to you, but I see a lot of guys who don't follow it when they paint their properties. Too many Landlords use a half-inch or one-fourth-inch paint sleeve, either because they don't realize it takes forever to get paint on the walls with a skinny sleeve, or because they're too cheap to spend an extra two bucks on a thicker sleeve.

Both reasons sound foolish to me. The one-and-one-fourth-inch sleeves are the only way to go! For the extra two bucks that you'll spend on them, you'll get the paint on the walls in half the time. This thicker sleeve is going to hold a lot more paint. And the more paint that a sleeve holds, the less time you'll spend reloading it— dipping it back into the bucket. Additionally, you won't have to back-roll as much, meaning you won't have to re-roll over your work.

In short, having more paint on the sleeve is going to put more paint on the wall, which in turn means more coverage. So, the thicker the sleeve, the faster the job gets done!

Thicker sleeves hold more paint.

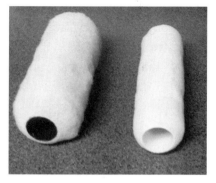

See the difference?

TIP 34

Do Not Let
Your Tenants Paint

As soon as your Tenants move in, they will most likely ask you if they can paint the walls. Early on, when I didn't have any experience, I would give them permission to paint if they wished. I figured that if they took the initiative to paint the place, maybe they would take care of it.

Fortunately, 95 percent of the Tenants who asked if they could paint did not follow through with their requests. The other 5 percent must have been colorblind. Never did I think they would paint the walls violet, pink, cherry, or black. I think they got their color schemes from the side of a water-ice truck! I've had to stain-kill walls as many as five times before the colors would stop bleeding through. And not only that, the Tenants got paint all over the carpets and then had the gall to ask for new ones because, "The old ones have paint all over them."

So, always say, "No way" to paint! Tell Tenants that the colors on the walls when they move in need to be the same when they move out. I also put it into my leases that Tenants are not to paint or wallpaper anything in the house, because let me tell you, removing wallpaper is another fun chore. If they do either, my lease lets me evict them for a lease violation.

TIP 35

Make Sure the
Interior Doors are Solid

If you purchase an older home and begin rehabbing it, leave the solid bedroom and closet doors in place. Do whatever it takes to get them swinging and closing properly. If you have to add an eight dollar doorknob to get them to close correctly, do it. Why? Because the newer, hollow doors suck! They may swing gracefully for twenty years in your house or mine, but they ain't gonna last long in a rental property. Think about it. If your Tenants are fighting between themselves and one of them locks him or herself in a bedroom, it won't take much for the other to kung fu the door down!

Now, let's say one of the doors must be replaced because it's either beyond repair or was totally missing from the property when you made the settlement. Don't try to save a buck by purchasing a

pre-hung hollow door. If you do, you'll end up paying more in the long run because you'll have to replace it again and again. Spend the extra thirty dollars and get a door with a solid core. That way, instead of breaking the door in an attempt to knock it down, the Tenant will either break his or her hand, the eight dollar doorknob will give way, or the hinges will pull out. You can always re-hinge a solid-core door. But unless your Tenant's name is Bruce Lee, he's not gonna splinter the door or punch a hole through it! I can guarantee you that.

Door with a solid core.

TIP 36

Use Structo-Lite
to Repair Basement Walls

If your basement walls are all solid concrete, then lucky you! You don't have to do anything and your walls will last forever. Unfortunately, that is rarely the case in older houses. The basement walls in older homes are usually made of dirt, clay, and plaster. When the plaster covering the walls gets old, it starts to deteriorate. Then, the dirt or clay behind the plaster falls to the floor, which lets you know that something must be done to patch the walls and stop them from crumbling.

This is where my tip comes in. It will save you a ton of money and a lot of time. As far as I can tell, 99 percent of the investors in

Deteriorated basement wall.

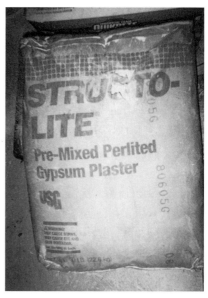

Bag of Structo-Lite.

Wall patched with Structo-Lite.

this business use sand, lime, and cement to repair basement walls. But not me! Buying and mixing those items is expensive and very time consuming. Also, if you mix it too dry you'll lose half of it in the pan, and if you mix it too wet it falls off of the wall. You just can't win!

Instead, use the product that I use and you'll be a winner every time. It is called Structo-Lite and boy does it work! Not only is it cheaper and just as durable as the sand, lime, and cement mix, but it sticks to the walls better, mixes faster, and covers more area. It comes in fifty-pound bags and all you need to do is mix it with water until it has a peanut-buttery consistency, slap it on the walls, and you're done. The stuff dries as hard as iron. You can purchase it at Home Depot and I promise that it's worth every penny!

TIP 37
Install Dropped Ceilings

Let's say you purchase a home and the ceilings are a wreck! The drywall or plaster has holes in it, the ceilings are stained, or there are a number of other problems.

You now have a decision to make. Do you fix the ceilings the expensive and time consuming way, or the fast and inexpensive way? Well, the reason you purchased this book was to save cash, and you should know me well enough by now to know which one I'm gonna pick. That's right, the fast and cheap way! Let me go ahead and explain both to you, though.

First I'll tell you about the expensive and time consuming way. It involves ripping down the old, destroyed drywall or lath, cutting and hanging new drywall, spackling and taping your joints not once, but twice, and then putting two coats of paint on the ceiling. There's nothing wrong with it, but it takes too much damn time! You have to come back at least three different days while you wait for the spackle to dry, and then you have to wait for the first coat of paint to dry before you can put on the second. That's not even mentioning the clean-up each and every time! I'm sure it will look great once you're done, but do you really have the time? Remember, every day your property sits vacant is a day that you lose rental income.

Now it's time to learn about the cheap and inexpensive way. Install a dropped ceiling! It's the fastest and easiest way to go, not to mention the cleanest. You don't have to worry about paint spilling or spackle dust from sanding going all over the house. All you need to do is simply remove the hanging debris from the ceiling and install your dropped ceiling.

Dropped ceilings come in four parts and can be installed in four steps. The first step is placing the wall angle around the complete perimeter of the room, about eight inches below the existing ceiling. Next, the main runners, which are spaced four feet apart vertically and span the length of the room, need to be installed. The third step involves placing the tee's two feet apart horizontally all around the room. And finally, the four feet by two feet tiles need to be snapped into place to complete the project. The whole process should take you about three hours for one room. And the more you do it, the faster you will get. I could probably snap one together in an average-sized bedroom in about an hour and a half. Plus, they're pretty inexpensive!

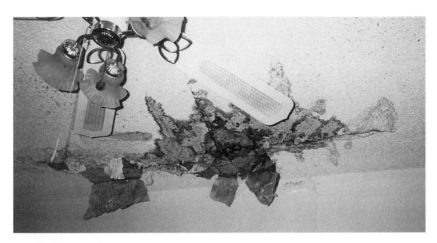

Damaged ceilings.

Dropped ceiling in a bedroom.

Dropped ceiling in a living room.

TIP 38

Limit Damage Caused by Leaks and Floods

Although there is no surefire way to prevent leaks or floods from happening, there is a way to limit the damage that they cause. I used to feel like choking my Tenants when they'd call and say that their toilet broke and was now overflowing. I'd fly over to the property only to discover that, 99 percent of the time, the toilet wasn't broken, it was clogged! And there my clueless Tenants would stand, just watching the water continue to destroy my property. If they would have just turned off the water from the toilet, they would have prevented everything but the clog! Instead, due to their inaction, my ceiling would be stained if not ruined, my carpets would be soaked, and the floor boards under them would soon start to twist like pretzels. And somehow, the Tenants would always have the gall to tell me that it wasn't their fault!

Fortunately, I have come up with a surefire way to stop the damage that leaks and floods inflict. I've also come up with a surefire way to make any and all damage that does result from floods the Tenants' fault. Lucky for you, I'm going to tell you how!

In every property I own, I have my plumber install a ball valve to the main water supply line, which is usually located in the basement of the property. As you can see by the picture on page 83, a four-year-old would know how to turn the water off and on. Then, the day my Tenants move in, I walk them directly down to the basement and show them where the ball valve is and how to use it. I also tell them that if they don't turn the water off the minute there is a leak or flood emergency, then they will be held fully responsible for all the damages!

Additionally, I make the Tenants sign an addendum to the lease that says the same thing that I just told them. Here is what the addendum looks like:

Flood Addendum

In the event of a flood, Tenant agrees that Landlord has shown and told Tenant how to turn off main water valve in leased property.

Tenant agrees to turn main water valve off immediately in case of an emergency such as an overflowing toilet, burst water supply line, burst washer hose line, burst hot water heater, etc.

Tenant will always turn off main valve during an emergency before calling the Landlord or a plumber.

Tenant agrees that if no one will be occupying the property for more than 48 hours, such as in the case of vacation or going away for the weekend, s/he will turn the main water valve off before vacating the property.

Should Tenant ignore flooding and not protect Landlord's property to the best of his or her ability, Tenant agrees that s/he will and should be responsible for any and all damages caused by flood.

Landlord Signature   Tenant Signature

Date   Date

Since I've incorporated these two techniques, I haven't had any Tenants call me and tell me that they have Niagara Falls coming down in the middle of the living room. You will be pleasantly surprised at how well making your Tenants accountable for certain things works! Trust me.

Main ball valve in
open position.

Main ball valve in
closed position.

TIP 39

Prevent Roaches
without an Exterminator

I cannot stand roaches! They are filthy and disgusting creatures. Some people say that God put everything on the face of this earth for a reason. Well, if His reason for roaches was to annoy the hell out of Landlords, He hit the nail on the head.

All Landlords are going to run into a roach problem at least once in their lives. When you do, the experience can be enough to drive you nuts! You send an exterminator over to the property one day and the roaches are back the next. Meanwhile, your Tenant continues to call and demand that the exterminator come back. So, not only is the Tenant bothering you, but every time the exterminator has to re-spray the property you lose money. Is there any way to prevent this problem from happening to you? You bet!

For ten years I chased those little S.O.B.'s around with exterminators and Raid, which turned out to be just a big waste of money. After the exterminator sprayed, I'd do a body count and see about ten of them upside down on their backs, but I would venture to guess that about a hundred others got away. Where did they go? Directly underneath the baseboards and in between the walls is where. The roach spray cannot reach all the way between the walls, so the roaches just sit tight, wait for the spray to dry, and then come right back out again. They may be filthy bugs, but they are not *stupid*, filthy bugs. They have survived for millions of years and they even say that if there is ever a nuclear war, roaches will be the only species that survives.

Okay, so if they are so smart, how did I figure out a way to prevent them? Experience—what else?! A row home that I once owned was right next door to another Landlord-owned property. The fellow that owned the home next to mine was 78 years old, had been a Landlord for over 50 years, and was as sharp as a tack. One day he saw me going into my property with a can of Raid in my hand. "Roaches, huh?" he asked. "Yeah," I said. "You're wasting your money. That stuff barely burns their eyes," he replied. "Oh, really? What do you have, a secret roach spray?" I joked. "No," he said, "but what I do have is a secret that'll prevent you from ever seeing another roach in your life." Now he had me intrigued and I was all ears. "From day one, you've got to prevent them from ever getting into your house, and there's only one way to do it—Borax!"

I won't keep giving you the he said, I said end of it, but I will tell you exactly what he told me to do and it worked like a charm. It's very, very, simple and it will make you scratch your head and say, "Geez, why didn't I think of that?"

This procedure should be done when you first purchase a property, before you ever rent it out. What's great about this tip is that you only have to do it once, and then you're good for the rest of the time you own that property. First, you need to purchase Borax roach powder or crystals. Then, with a brick-pointing tool or small putty knife, press the Borax powder as far under the baseboards as you can get it. Do this throughout the entire house. Next, caulk between the baseboards and floor to seal the roach poison between the walls. And finally, remove your exterminator's phone number from your cell phone because you won't need it anymore!

This process establishes a boundary around your home that roaches will not cross. Typically, they live and breed between the walls of your property, but by sealing the walls off with caulk, you are preventing the roaches from getting behind them. Also, you are lacing the walls with poison that roaches can smell for miles and will not want to get anywhere near. Like I said, I didn't learn this tip until about four years ago, so I've wasted hundreds of dollars on Raid and thousands of dollars on exterminator service calls. Luckily, you can learn from my mistakes and save a couple hundred bucks and a good bit of your sanity!

TIP 40
Purchase these
Life-Saving Tools

I won't get too carried away with talking about tools for two reasons. The first is because I could talk about them all day, and the second is because it's not likely that anyone would switch from what they're using to what I'm using anyway. Tools cost money, so if I said I only use a Dewalt screw gun, are you going to throw away your Makita screw gun and run out and get a Dewalt? No, of course you're not. (For those of you who answered yes, I now have you brainwashed. Please send all of your money directly to me . . .)

However, there are two, inexpensive tools that I am going to recommend that you get. The first is the Husky Razor Knife, which only costs about eight dollars. Over the past twenty years I have put down thousands of stick-down tile floors. I used to use the old utility knives, which worked terrifically but caused a huge pain in my neck when it came time for me to change the blades. A screwdriver was needed to take them apart, and then the blades and the dispenser had to be lined up perfectly before they could be put back together. If they were off by even just a little bit, the whole thing would have to be taken apart again. I hated to get rolling on a floor only to have to stop and change a blade. Half of the time I would finish the floor with a blade that was only as sharp as a butter knife just so I wouldn't have to stop!

Now, I fortunately no longer have that problem because Husky has come out with a razor knife that is awesome! You can change out a blade in about twenty seconds without a screwdriver and without having to line up a damn thing. When the knife is open, it has a safety feature that locks the blade in place, and it even comes

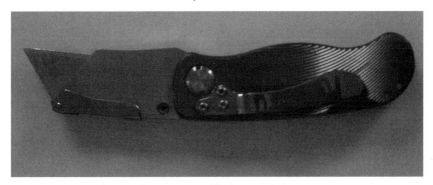

The Husky Razor Knife is a real time saver.

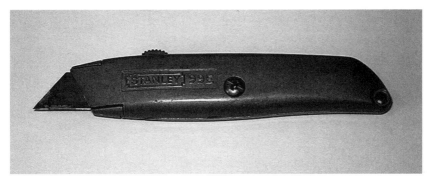

It was a real headache to change out the blades in old utility knives.

with a mounted clip so you can attach it to your belt or pocket. This knife is very slick and it is a real time saver.

The second tool I am recommending is the Jet Swet, which costs about thirty dollars. I do a lot of soldering, so I don't know how I ever lived without this tool! It's clever, easy to use, and will save you a ton of time.

Have you ever been in the basement of your home and had to replace a shut-off valve, but couldn't get the back-flow of water to stop trickling through it long enough to solder it? You probably tried some of the old tricks like stuffing a piece of bread into the line or tilting the line upward to cut off the flow of water. These never really work, though, and you end up rattling off about a hundred of the foulest curse words in the book. Shortly after that, you throw down your torch and decide to just wait an hour for the entire house to drain down, which not only takes time, but also leaves you with a soaking wet basement floor.

There's now a fast and easy solution, though! Jet Swet has come up with the greatest plumbing invention since PVC. What you do is simply insert one end into your half-inch line, and then tighten the nut on the back to expand the rubber and cut off the back-flow of water. Then, just sweat on your new shut-off valve, remove your Jet Swet, and call it a day. No more cursing, waiting, or wet floors.

Jet Swet sells this tool in all different sizes; however, I have only had to use the half-inch and three-fourths-inch varieties. For directions, pricing, and ordering information, go to www.brenelle.com. I know I say that a half-inch Jet Swet costs thirty bucks and they say forty, but I assure you that I purchased mine at my local plumbing-supply house for thirty, so I'm sure you can do the same.

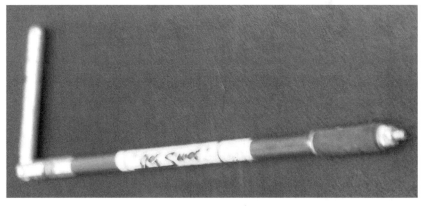

Jet Swet tool.

EXTERIOR
WORK

TIP 41

Do Not Grant Tenants Access to the Garage

Garages and Tenants are like oil and water. No matter how hard you try, they don't mix! Tenants will think of a hundred things to do with a garage, none of which involve parking a car in it. For example, I once had a Tenant running a car repair shop out of the garage! He had a big, wooden sign spray painted with the name of his business and a big arrow that directed cars up the driveway.

I had another guy running a furniture store out of the garage. He would go trash picking, and then sell the junk and old furniture out of the garage. It looked like *Sanford and Son* outside of my rental! I've also had many Tenants turn the garage into another bedroom. I once even had a guy turn the garage into a "Gold's Gym." He sold memberships to join and everything! I even had a call from License and Inspections one time, because the person who was living in one of my homes was conducting dog fighting matches in the garage.

And if the Tenants aren't using the garage for business or living space, they are busy trashing it, literally! I can't tell you how many times a Tenant moved out, and then, when I opened the garage door, I said, "What the hell!" It always seemed like there was more trash and rubble left in that 10 foot by 15 foot space than there was in the entire home. I was then stuck with clearing everything out of the garage and spending my hard-earned money on dumping fees to get rid of the Tenant's trash.

If I thought about it for a little while longer, I'm sure I could come up with 100 other wrongful uses for a garage. However, I'm sure that by now you get my point. So, the question is what to do if your property has a garage attached to it. First of all, take the garage out of the lease. You've got to let your Tenants know that they are not permitted into the garage for any reason. Here is an addendum that I have my Tenants sign before they move into one of my properties:

Garage Addendum

I _____,
the Tenant, know and agree that the garage of the unit I am renting is not included in this lease. I agree I am to have no access to this section (the garage) of the property that I am renting.

I agree not to tamper with any locks on the garage or to try and gain access to the garage by any other means.

I understand and agree that the Landlord can, will, and should evict me if I, or any other member of this household, enter or disturb the garage.

_____   _____
Landlord Signature   Tenant Signature

_____   _____
Date   Date

Eliminating the garage from the lease was not a problem for me, and now it won't be a problem for you. However, here *is* the problem! If you let somebody rent a house from you and you tell them not to enter a padlocked door, they're going to enter anyway, or at the very least, try like hell to enter. Whether they tear the padlock off of the door or remove the hinge pins, they're going to do their best to get in. I used to even show them that there was nothing in the garage, but still, curiosity would get the best of them. Well, either curiosity or the simple fact that I told them to "stay the hell out of there."

As I mentioned, the first thing I did in an attempt to keep Tenants out of the garage was to add a padlock to each side of the door. This only had a success rate of about 60 percent, though, because some Tenants would rip it off.

Padlocked garage door. You can see where the hasp
was already pried off!

The next thing I did brought me up to a 100 percent success rate. I eliminated the entire garage door, and then added a pre-hung steel door and sided over top of the existing plywood. Below are some before and after pictures:

Go from this nasty, old garage door with broken windows . . .

. . . to this clean-looking, sided rear door.

The entire ordeal should cost you around $300 and take about six hours to finish. If you're thinking to yourself, "Why should I waste three hundred bucks doing that? I'll just leave the garage door as it stands," consider the following reasons. First, if you don't do it, every single time a Tenant moves out you'll be wasting countless hours and dollars on clean outs and dumping fees. Second, many of these old garage doors have anywhere from four to ten windows. They always get broken and your Tenants will be calling you to come out and fix them. And if it's not your Tenants calling, it will be building inspectors. Additionally, take a look at the pictures of the unrepaired garage doors. They are infested with lead-based paint. Once you eliminate the door, you also eliminate the lead-based paint. And finally, by neatly eliminating the garage door, your property will look a lot nicer, which in turn should make it that much easier to rent.

Garage windows can get broken, leading to failed inspections.

Another neatly eliminated garage door!

Believe me; I hate spending money as much as, if not more than the next guy. I paid too many times to consider giving my Tenants access to the garage anymore, though. The $300 upfront is worth it! Once you eliminate the garage, you never have to clean so much as a cigarette butt out of it, or spend another nickel on this area of the home again!

TIP 42

Choose Rubber over Tar Roofs

If you have a flat roof that needs to be replaced, a roofer is going to give you two choices—tar or rubber. Always choose rubber! Rubber will last for as long as you own the property. All you have to do is coat it every four or five years and you're good to go. Tar roofs, on the other hand, start to blister very early on, and no way will they last you as long as a rubber roof. Yes, the rubber will cost you about $200 more initially, but in the long-term it is well worth the investment.

I'll be honest with you, 99 percent of the houses I own or have owned have flat roofs. So, while I wish I could give you some advice on shingle and slate roofs, I can't. All of this book's great information and advice comes from what I know through first-hand experience. I will never give you any guesswork!

Rubber roofs are a great investment.

TIP 43
Cover Windows
with Plywood and Siding

Most houses have several windows—sometimes up to twelve of them! This is a Landlord's worst nightmare, because if all of the windows are old, wooden, inoperable, and have chipped paint, they will all have to be replaced, right? Wrong! Houses only need one operable window for ventilation, so just replace one of them. You can simply cover the others with plywood and siding.

One window costs about $140, whereas a piece of half-inch plywood that will cover two or three windows only costs $20. Not only that, once you eliminate a window, you eliminate all chances of it ever getting broken again. There will no longer be any baseballs smashing through it, any broken balancers or window locks, any easy break-ins, or any window-related problems in general—ever!

You can use this trick on just about any window that you don't feel like spending big bucks on. Check out the pictures. I have done

Six porch windows eliminated.

it to bedroom windows, dining room windows, enclosed-porch windows, and basement windows (more on basement windows in the next tip). It works like a charm!

Two bedroom windows and four porch windows eliminated.

Two porch windows eliminated.

Three basement windows and five first floor windows eliminated.

TIP 44
Replace Remaining Basement Window with a Hopper

I don't know what it is about basement windows, but Tenants love to break 'em! Then, once the window is broken, the Tenants never want to take responsibility for the damage. The typical broken basement window scenario usually plays out something like this: Your Tenants somehow manage to lock themselves out of the property. They don't want to pay a lock-out fee or kick in the front door, so what happens? One of their feet goes right through the basement window! They scoot through it, let themselves in, and go upstairs.

Then, you get this phone call: "Mike, you've got to get over here. Somebody (usually a kid playing ball in the street) broke my basement window and I need you to fix it." Since the basement window is at street level, they think you'll buy their story. Wrong!

First of all, my lease has a window waiver saying I am not responsible for any broken windows, including those in the basement, no matter who broke them or how it was done. You should include one in your lease, too. But even if you do, I can tell you from experience that you're still going to get the crazy story and an argument anyway.

Eliminate the story and the argument by eliminating basement windows! As discussed in the previous tip, if the basement windows in your rental property are old and need to be replaced, only replace one of them. Leave the one for some ventilation and seal the rest of them off with plywood and siding.

Since 99 percent of activity occurs in front of the house—not out back—the back basement window is the one that you want to keep. Replace whatever type of window is in there now with a hopper. They are inexpensive—about $40—and you can frame them and stick them into just about any sized basement window opening. The hoppers are smaller than regular-sized windows, and the smaller the window, the smaller the chances of it getting broken!

Sealed off basement window in the front of the house.

Installed hopper window in the back of the house.

TIP 45
Cover the Porch Ceiling
with Vinyl Siding

If your property has a front or rear porch, look up at its ceiling. If the paint is chipping or peeling—and it usually is—something has to be done. Luckily, I have the perfect solution. Side it!

That's right, the same vinyl siding and J-channel joints that are typically used on the sides of houses, can also be used on porch ceilings. It looks great when finished and you'll never have to paint the ceiling again in your life!

Porch ceiling before siding

Porch ceiling after siding.

It would cost you about forty bucks for the gallon of paint and other supplies you'd need to paint the ceiling. To side a ceiling you'll need about sixty dollars worth of material, but you'll never have to do it again. So, although it's more money upfront, it's a great investment. Additionally, anyone can do siding. It's that easy. Just screw the J-channel around the perimeter of the surface that you want to side, cut the siding with shears, snap it into place, and you're done.

TIP 46
Do Not Install
or Repair Screens

I will tell you right up front that I don't install or repair screens, because they are repeat offenders. They are a repair that always comes back, again and again. It's not like putting a new steel door on your property and never getting a service call about it again. No. With screens, Tenants will call you every spring like clockwork to tell you that six or seven are ripped and need to be replaced. They'll act like the air outside is toxic and claim they can't breathe it unless there is a screen in place.

First of all, the reason for the screens getting ripped is that some Tenants don't know how to take care of them. They follow the theory, "We rip 'em, you fix 'em." I'm having none of it! I've lived in my present home for nine years and I kid you not, I haven't had to replace one screen. So, I don't believe Tenants for one second when they tell me that their screens just ripped on their own.

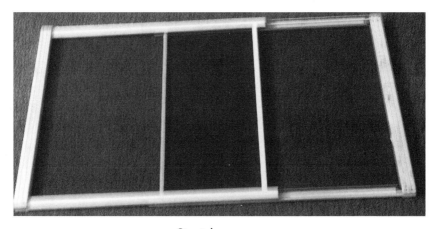

Stretch screen.

Installed stretch screen.

I put it in my leases that I'm not responsible for screens in any way, shape, or form. I did get stuck once, though. I needed to have screens in place in a property I purchased outside of Philadelphia in order to be granted a Use and Occupancy (U/O) certificate. Well, the house had thirty windows and not one screen! I called a window company and had a guy come out to the house to measure the windows and give me an estimate for the cost of window screens. He told me $900! That's right, $30 per screen. I almost had a heart attack.

What did I do to avoid spending this fortune? First, I told the window company guy to get off of my property. Then, I went to Home Depot and purchased stretch screens. They only cost $10 apiece, so right off the bat the savings were tremendous. Plus, there was no measuring needed and I didn't have to wait for the screens to be made. The final bonus was how easy they were to install! I simply had to stretch the screen from side to side and I was done—for a third of the price. So, avoid screens whenever possible. But if you must install them, use stretch screens and install them yourself.

TIP 47
Remove All Shrubbery

Be sure to eliminate all bushes, hedges, small trees, and other shrubbery from the front and rear of your property. By eliminate, I mean cut them down as far as possible. The reason for this is that even though my leases state that lawn care is the Tenants' responsibility, a lot of times they don't bother and the shrubbery becomes overgrown.

Your home does not have to look like a well-landscaped golf course for someone to rent it. However, if the bushes, hedges, and trees are overgrown, you may receive violations from the city or township inspectors. If you eliminate everything that you can before the Tenant moves in, it will help out tremendously.

Before eliminating shrubbery.

After eliminating shrubbery.

TIP 48
Make Tenants
Responsible for Oil Heaters

Oil heaters—I hate 'em! They're dirty, usually very old, and always break down. Trying to find someone who knows how to fix them and is willing to do so is another treat! Unfortunately, if you purchase a home with an oil heater already in it, you are stuck with it. That is unless you want to pay someone to rip it out and replace it with a gas heater. I'm a little too cheap to do that, though, and it's my guess that you feel the same way. Luckily, there is one Tenant-related oil heater repair that can be prevented with a simple addendum to the lease.

In typical scenarios, when Tenants run out of oil they call for a delivery. The oil company will make the delivery and be on their merry way. The problem, however, is that when the Tenant goes to turn on the heat there still won't be any. That is because once the system runs dry, it needs to be "primed" so that it can start sucking oil through it again.

The oil company would have primed it for about twenty bucks while they were out there if the Tenants had asked. But instead, you've got the Tenants on the phone with you telling you that the heater is broken! When you tell them they need to call the oil company again and spend the money to get it primed, they don't want to hear it. They don't want to spend another cent and they think it is your responsibility to get the heater up and running.

I soon got totally sick of this phone call, so I added this addendum to my lease:

Oil Heating Systems Addendum

Tenant agrees not to let oil tank drop below $^1/_8$ of a tank.

Tenant agrees that s/he will be responsible for any and all repairs to the heating system should the oil tank run dry.

Tenant agrees that s/he will be responsible for the cost of priming the system should the oil tank run dry.

Tenant agrees not to heat the home or unit with any source other than the heater.

Landlord is giving possession of the property to the Tenant with _____ (amount) of oil in the tank. Tenant agrees to return the property to the Landlord with at least the same amount. If the tank is below this amount, the Tenant will be charged accordingly.

_____   _____
Landlord Signature   Tenant Signature

_____   _____
Date   Date

TIP 49
Switch to Cheaper Plywood

When rehabbing your property, you are always going to need plywood somewhere for something. For years I had been using the expensive plywood, because I figured that if I was closing off porch or basement windows with it, I might as well use the good stuff. I didn't want to come back in two years and find the plywood rotting away.

But then, several winters ago, I hired an out-of-work union carpenter to help me with an enclosed porch. It had nine windows that I wanted to plywood and side over. When he pulled his truck into the shop to load up the materials, he asked, "Mike, why are you using this stuff?" Intrigued, I told him to enlighten me and tell me what I should be using instead.

He told me that the half-inch plywood I was using costs around fifteen dollars per sheet, which is true. He then told me to instead use the OSB five-eighths-inch plywood, which only costs ten dollars per sheet—especially since all I was doing was covering windows with it. Still skeptical, I asked, "Yeah, but won't it eventually rot out?" "Hell no!" he said. "That's all they're using in new construction these days and you don't see any new houses falling down do you? You'll be long gone or dead by the time this wood rots out."

Well, it doesn't take much to talk me into saving a buck, so I switched to the cheaper plywood so fast it would make your head spin. After all, OSB plywood is a little thicker than the regular plywood, his idea made sense, he had twenty-three years of experience, and I love saving cash. I can't understand why people are frightened of change or new ideas. I'll tell you what—I'm actually frightened of the old ones!

We switched from this expensive plywood . . .

. . . to this cheaper plywood.

TIP 50
Patch Concrete Sidewalks before Inspection

Let me tell you about a life- and money-saving product that I have been using for years. I came across it because every so often I would get a city inspector who would harass me over a couple of spider-web cracks on the sidewalk. The cracks weren't big enough for someone to trip over, yet he would hold up my Use and Occupancy certificate until something was done about them. I didn't want to rip out the entire cement block and replace it, because that would cost anywhere from $150 to $200. But on the other hand, if nothing was done about the cracks I wouldn't be able to move any Tenants into the property.

The answer to my dilemma was Quickrete Vinyl Concrete Patcher! A bag only costs about twelve dollars, it easily mixes with water, it has no stones in it so it goes on smoothly, and it will certainly get you your Use and Occupancy certificate. I don't take chances anymore. Before calling city inspectors out for the final inspection of my properties, I repair every single crack with this product and you should do the same. You don't need an inspector failing you for something as asinine as a small crack on a cement block.

Quickrete Vinyl
Concrete Patcher.

Conclusion

Fifty tips later, we've finally reached the end of the book. I sincerely hope that you are able to put some of my advice to good use. If you do, you will save much more money than what this book put you out—I am sure of it! Every single dollar you save will go or stay directly in your bank account. And after all, making and saving money is the reason you decided to get into the business of real estate investing in the first place, correct?

Like I said in the beginning, I did not just come up with these tips off the top of my head; every single one began as a problem, but soon became a well thought out solution. Lucky for you, Landlording is a field where you can actually purchase experience. It's not like being a policeman or a teacher, where you have to be in the field yourself to gain experience. No, with Landlording, if someone who has been in the field for ten years tells you to go with hardwood floors instead of carpeting, it's a pretty good bet that hardwood floors are the way to go. Although you'll never stop learning in this business—I've been in it for years and I'm still learning—I just gave your career a jump start with fifty of my most valuable tips!

If you are smart, it is relatively easy to succeed in the field of real estate investing. You find a house or apartment, fix it up, and get it rented. There's really not much more to it than that. Money- and time-saving tips will definitely help you along the way, but you've got to be dedicated and motivated if you really want to make it happen. So, when a problem comes along, stay positive, use this book, and think a little outside the box. If you do, you'll figure out a way to not only fix the issue you're facing, but also prevent it from ever happening to you again!

I would like to begin writing another book of fifty tips that can help Landlords, but in order to do so I'll need some class participation, so to speak. I've shared my tips with you; now I'm asking you to share your tips with me! If you think you have a tip or idea that can save Landlords time and/or money, email me at section8bible@yahoo.com, and I'll do my best to get your tip into my next book. Be sure to include your name and where you are from, so that I can attribute your advice. In the meantime, I sincerely hope you enjoyed and learned from this book, and good luck to you!

Index

Addendum, 5
  Broken Window, 6
  Flood, 82
  Garage, 92
  Oil Heating Systems, 109
  See also Lease.
Advertising your property,
  44–45
Air conditioner, window-unit,
  60–61
Answering machine, 27
Appraisals, 17

Background check, 41–42
  supplementary, for Tenants,
  42
Bake, 58
Ball valve, 81, 83.
Bank, 15–17
  foreclosure, 49
Banker, 17
Basement
  main water supply located in
  the, 28, 81–83
  walls, 76–77
  windows, 99–101
Bathroom, 62–66
  faucets, 63
  shower curtains, 65

showers, 64–65
sinks, 62–64
toilet overflowing in the, 81
tubs, 63–65
vanities, 62
Bathtub faucets, 63
Battleship, Navy, 71
Bedroom
  doors, 75
  eliminating, windows, 99
  installing a dropped ceiling
  in a, 79–80
Bierce, Ambrose, 21
Blades, changing, 67, 86–87
Blanket mortgage, 15–17
Blown fuses, 60
Borax roach powder, 85
Break-ins, *See* Theft.
Broil, 58
Broken window, 5–7, 60, 94–95,
  98, 100–101
Broken Window Addendum,
  5–6
Brute trash cans, 50–51
Building inspectors, *See*
  Inspectors, city and
  building.
Bulbs, light, 53

Bulletproof Landlord Lease,
7–8. *See also* Lease.
Burners, stove, 58
Bushes, *See* Shrubbery.

Can,
carpet in a, 71
trash, 50–51
Carpenter, 110
Carpet
bar, 67
in a can, 71
cleaners, 69
as a drop cloth, 70, 74
hardwood flooring
underneath, 70–71
installing, 66, 69–70
investing in, 70
Caulk, 64, 85
Ceiling fans, 53–55
Ceilings
damaged, 78–79
dropped, 78–80
porch, 102–103
Cell phone, *See* Personal phone
number.
Cement, *See* Concrete.
Ceramic tile, *See* Tile, ceramic.
Chandeliers, 53
Christmas, 58, 69
Christmas Eve, 58
City inspectors, *See* Inspectors,
city and building.
Clean-out companies, 49–50
Cleaning out properties, *See*
Property clean-out.
Cleanliness, Tenant, 33–34
Clogging the sink, 56, 59

Closet doors, 75
Cockroaches, *See* Roaches.
Collateral, 17
Colton, Charles, 21
Concrete
basement walls, 76–77
sidewalks, 112
Consolidation, loan, 15–16
Contractors, *See* Workers.
Cosmetic repairs, 32, 37, 66
Court, 5, 9, 10, 12, 53, 57
Courtroom, 9, 11
Cracks, sidewalk, 112
Credit check form, 46
Credit line, 15. *See also* Credit
score.
Credit score, 16. *See also* Credit
line.
Criminal background check, 41–42
Curtains, shower, 65

Dewalt screw gun, 86
Dishes, doing, 59
Dishwasher, 59
Disposal, garbage, 56–57, 59
Document
important, 19
preparation fee, 17
See also Legal document.
Door hinges, 75
Doorknob, 75
Doors
bedroom, 75
closet, 75
hollow, 75
lock the, 37, 44
do not open, 38
solid-core, 75

Dropped ceiling, 78–80
Drywall, 78
Dumping trash, 50, 52, 91, 95
Dumpster, 52

Electric stove, 58
Electrical
  fire, 72
  outlet, 60, 72
  problems, 72
  switch, 72
  upgrades, 72
Electrician, 61, 72
Electronic igniters in gas
  stoves, 58
Eliminating items from the
  property, 49, 52–57, 59–62,
  93–96, 98–101, 106–107
Emergency
  repair, 27
  situation, 28, 81–82
Eviction, 9, 28, 33, 69, 74, 92
Evidence, 9–12
Exterminator, 84–85

Fans, ceiling, 53–55
Faucets, 63
Fees
  document preparation, 17
  dumping, 91, 95
  writing, 17
  credit check, 17
Files, 19
Filing cabinet, 19
Financial organization, 15, 17
Fire, 28
  electrical, 72
Fixtures, light, 53, 55, 72

Flat roof, 97
Flood Addendum, 82
Floods, 28, 81–83. *See also* Leaks.
Floors,
  bathroom, 66–67
  hardwood, 70–71
  kitchen, 66–68
  painting the, 71
  See also Carpet.
Florescent lights, 53
Footing ladders, 40
For rent signs, 44–45
Foreclosure, 49
Franklin, Ben, 18, 21
Fuses, blown, 60

Garage
  Addendum, 92
  attempting to enter the, 93
  denying Tenants access to
    the, 92–96
  Tenants trashing the, 91
  use of the, 92
  wrongful uses for a, 91
Garage doors
  eliminating, 94–96
  locks on, 92–93
Garbage
  disposal, 56–57
  removal, 49–52
Gas heaters, 108
Gas stove, 58
Gold's Gym, 91
Good Tenants, *See* Tenants, good.
Ground fault interrupter, 72

Hampton Bay ceiling fan, 53
Hanging shower curtains, 65

Hardwood floors, 70–71
Headache, save yourself a, 41,
   56, 59, 63
Heaters
   gas, 108
   oil, 108–109
Heating elements in electric
   stoves, 58
Hedges, *See* Shrubbery.
Hinge pins, 93
Hinges, door, 75
Holiday, 58
Hollow door, 75
Home Depot, 50, 53, 55, 66–67,
   77, 105. *See also* Home-
   improvement stores.
Home-improvement stores, 72.
   See also Home Depot.
Home phone, *See* Personal
   phone number.
Hooks, installing, for
   organization, 20
Hopper, 100–101
Husky Razor Knife, 86–87

Images stick-down tiles, 67
Income, *See* Rent.
Injuries, 38, 40–41. *See also*
   Mugged, getting.
Injury, risk of, 53–57, 59, 71
Inspectors, city and building,
   37, 95, 106, 112. *See also*
   License and Inspections;
   Permits.
Insurance, 53, 57
   binder, 19
   carrier, 53, 60
Interest rate, average, 16–17

Investigative work, *See*
   Background check.

J-Channel, 102–103
Jet Swet, 87–88
Joints, 78, 102–103
Judge, 9–12
   pro-Tenant, 5, 7

Kant, Immanuel, 21
Kennedy, Florence, 21
Kennedy, John F., 21
Keyboard, 18–19
Keys to your properties,
   18–19
Kitchen floors, 66–68
Knife, 64
   Husky Razor, 86–87
   utility, 86–87
Knives, *See* Knife.

Ladder, 40
Landlord business, 5, 15, 23,
   29–30, 33, 49, 56, 62
Landlord, deny being the, 39
Landscaping, 106
Lath, 78
Lawn care, 106
Lawsuit, 60, 71
Lawyer, 53
Lead-based paint, 95. *See also*
   Paint; Painting.
Leaks, 59, 63–65, 81. *See also* Floods.
Lease
   bulletproof Landlord, 7–8
   getting the, signed, 42–43
   importance of a good, 5
   people named on the, 27–28

violation, 28, 74
what to include in the, 10–12,
28, 91–93, 100, 105–106
See also Addendum.
Legal document, 7. *See also*
Addendum; Lease.
Letterman, David, 69
License and Inspections, 91; *See
also* Inspectors, city and
building; Permits.
Light
bulbs, 53
fixtures, 53, 55, 72
Lights, florescent, 53
Linoleum, 66–67
Loan, 15–17
Locking doors, 37, 44
Locks, tampering with, 92–93
Luan, 66–67

Main water supply, 28
Makita screw gun, 86
Milne, A.A., 21
Mistakes, 23
Moen faucets, 63
Mopping, 70
Mortgage
blanket, 15–17
consolidation, 15–16
See also Loan.
Motivation, 23
Mugged, getting, 39–41. *See also*
Injuries.

Nails, underlayment, 67
Navy battleship, 71
Negotiating with banks, 17
Newman, John, 21

Newspaper advertisement, 44
No, say, *See* Say no.

Oil
company, 108
delivery, 108
heaters, 108–109
tank, 109
Oil Heating Systems
Addendum, 109
Open house, 46
Organizing
famous quotations about, 21
files, 19
finances, 15, 17
in general, 18–21
with hooks, 20
keys, 18–19
property showings, 46
Outlet
220, 60–12
electrical, 60, 72
Overflowing toilet, 81–82; *See
also* Floods; Leaks; Water
Damage.

Padlocks, *See* Locks, tampering
with.
Paint
do not let your Tenants, 74
lead-based, 95
oil-based, 71
Rust-Oleum, 71
sleeves, 73
See also Painting.
Painting
ceilings, 78, 103
the floors, 71

walls, 73–74
   See also Paint.
Peck, M. Scott, 21
Pegboard, 20
Penn, William, 21
Permits, 37, 52. *See also*
   Inspectors, city and
   building; License and
   Inspections.
Personal phone number, 27–28
Pet odor, 69
Phone book, 49
Phone conversations, 28
Photographs of the property,
   See Pictures.
Pick-up truck, *See* Truck, pick-
   up.
Pictures, 9–12
Pilots, stove, 58
Plaster, 76, 78
Plumber, 81–82
Plumbing invention, 88. *See also*
   Jet Swet.
Plywood, 94, 98, 100, 110–111
Porch
   ceilings, 102–103
   eliminating, windows, 99
Positive, remain, 23
Preventing injuries, 40–41, 46
Proof, *See* Evidence.
Property clean-out, 33, 49–52
Purchasing a property as is, 49

Qualifying Tenants, 43
Quikrete Vinyl Concrete
   Patcher, 112
Quotations, famous, about
   organization, 21

Raid, 84–85
Razorblade, 64, 67, 86–87
Recycling companies, 49–50, 52
Removing trash, *See* Trash
   removal.
Rent
   advertising your property is
      for, 44–45
   losing, because property is
      vacant, 78
   paying, 30–31
   Tenant got behind on the, 9
   worry about getting paid, 34
Rental application, 22, 46
Renting your property, 22, 34,
   39, 43–46, 95. *See also*
   Showing your property.
Repairs
   cosmetic, 32, 37
   emergency, 27
Restoring hardwood floors,
   70–71
Risk of injury, 53–57, 59, 71
Roaches, 84–85
Robbed, getting, *See* Mugged,
   getting.
Rod, shower, 65
Roof, 97
Rotting plywood, 110
Rubber roof, 97
Rubbish removal, *See* Trash
   removal.
Rust-Oleum paint, 71

Safety, your, 37–46
Sanding hardwood floors, 70
Sanford and Son, 91
Say no, 29–30, 61, 74

Scraper, razor, 64
Screens, 104–105
Screwdriver, 86
Seat tool, 63
Secondary phone line, 27
Section 8
    office, 40
    packet, 46
Security deposit, 22, 46
Shingle roof, 97
Shower curtains, 65
Showing your property, 22, 46.
    See also Renting your property.
Shrubbery, 106–107
Sidewalk cracks, 112
Siding, 94, 98, 100, 102–103, 110
Signature
    Landlord, 6, 82, 92, 109
    Tenant, 5–7, 9–12, 28, 82, 92,
        109
Single-handle faucets, 63
Sink
    bathroom, 62, 64
    clogging the, 56, 59
    faucets, 63
    trap, 62
    wall-mounted, 62
Slate roof, 97
Sleeves, paint, 73
Social security number, 41. *See
    also* Background check.
Soldering, 87. *See also* Jet Swet.
Solid-core door, 75
Spackle, 78
Stain-killing walls, 72. *See also*
    Paint; Painting.
Stake body truck, 52
Stealing, *See* Theft.

Stick-down tiles, *See* Tiles, stick-
    down.
Stove, 58
Stretch screens, 104–105
Structo-Lite, 76–77
Switch, electrical, 72

Tar roof, 97
Tenant
    background check, 42–43
    cleanliness, 33–34
    signature, 5–7, 9–12, 28, 82,
        92, 109
Tenants, good, 31, 42
Thanksgiving, 58
Theft, 37, 39, 44
Thieves, 37, 44
Three-handle faucets, 63
Tile
    ceramic, 66
    stick-down, 66–68, 86
    See also Floors.
Time, famous quotations about
    saving, 21
Toggle plate, 72
Toilet overflowing, 81–82. *See also*
    Floods; Leaks; Water Damage.
Tools, 37, 86–88
Trap, sink, 62
Trash cans, 50–51
Trash removal, 49–52, 91,
    95–96
Trees, *See* Shrubbery.
Truck, pick-up, 50–52
Tub, 63–64

Underlayment nails, 67
Upgrades

electrical, 72
property, 32
Use and Occupancy certificate,
  105, 112

Vacant property, 44–45, 78, 82
Vacuum, 69
Vanity, bathroom, 62
  See also Sink.
Varnishing hardwood floors, 70
Ventilation, 98, 100. *See also*
  Windows.
Video record the property, 12
Violating the lease, *See* Lease,
  violation.

Wall-mounted sink, 62
Wallpaper, 74. *See also* Paint;
  Painting.
Walls
  basement, 76–77

painting, 73–74
Water damage, 66, 70, 81–83.
  See also Floods; Leaks.
Water supply, main, 28, 81–83
Watching materials and tools, 37
Wax, hardwood floor, 70
Windows
  broken, 5–7, 60, 94–95, 98,
    100–101
  eliminating, 98–101
  installing screens in, 105
  outlets below, 60–61
  repairing, 5–6
  replacing, 98, 100–101
  waiver, 100
Window-unit air conditioners,
  60–61
Workers, 37–39
  hiring, 41–42
  paying, 50
  See also Background check.